One-a-Day

Pocket Stories: Rhymes, Riddles, and Reasons

What a treat to see *Rhymes, Riddles, and Reasons* being rewritten and reprinted as *One-A-Day Pocket Stories: Rhymes, Riddles, and Reasons*!

We started our weekly devotions every Monday night with our three children, Jonathan (now 28), Daniel (now 25), and Lindsey (now 22) when they were not even old enough to read! They loved every story and when they got a little older loved trying to figure out the riddles. We probably went through both volumes several times. The kids did not want to find another devotion book; they wanted to reread *Rhymes, Riddles, and Reasons*. I cannot wait to start reading this new one to our grandchildren.

When our son Jonathan and his wife requested a copy of *Rhymes, Riddles, and Reasons to start reading to their three children* for devotion, I discovered it was no longer in print. So, thank you, Barbara Westberg, for treating us with a new version! I know it will thrill many parents and children for years to come!

—Connie Bernard

One-a-Day

Pocket Stories: Rhymes, Riddles, and Reasons

Barbara Westberg

WORD AFLAME PRESS
HAZELWOOD, MO

One A Day Pocket Stories

by Barbara Westberg

© Copyright 2014 Barbara Westberg

Cover Design by Timothy Burk

Published by Word Aflame Press, 8855 Dunn Road, Hazelwood, MO 63042. Printed in the United States of America.

ISBN: 9781567229974

SKU: 25988

All Scripture quotations in this book are from the New King James Version of the Bible unless otherwise identified.

All rights reserved. No portion of this publication may be reproduced, stored in an electronic system or transmitted in any form or by any means, electronic, mechanical, photocopy, recording, or otherwise, without the prior permission of Word Aflame Press. Brief quotations may be used in literary reviews.

Library of Congress Cataloging-in-Publication Data

Westberg, Barbara.
 One-a-day pocket stories / Barbara Westberg.
    pages cm
 Includes bibliographical references and index.
 ISBN 978-1-56722-997-4 (alk. paper)
1. Families--Religious life. 2. Children--Religious life. 3. Devotional literature. I. Title.
  BV4526.3.W47 2014
  249--dc23
                           2014030889

Contents

Just a minute. 8
A Colorful Variety 11
In the Dark 14
The Creative Word 17
Only One Rule 20
The First Mistake 23
Side Effects 26
The Emergency Brake ... 29
The All-Seeing Eye 32
Best Friends 35
It's OK to Be Different 38
Get In 41
Not Forgotten 44
The Contract 47
The Control Tower 50
Flying in the Fog 53
The Cookie Jar 56
The Lead 59
Don't Rush It 62
Entertaining Strangers ... 65
Knock Again 68
Good News, Bad News ... 71
Just Wait 74
A New Home for Lowell ... 77
The Truce 80
Giving Till It Hurts 83
A Plot of Ground 86
Birds of a Feather 89
A New Life 92
Let's Trade 95
It Takes Two to Fight 98
Disguised 101
The Spoiled Brat 104
Afraid 107
Not Coincidence 110
The Cheater Cheated ... 113
Blessed Because 116
A Change of Plans 119
Making Peace 122
A New Name 125
The Rusty Box 128
No Expiration Date 132
The Comforter 135
It Takes Time 138
My Father's Favorite 141
Danny's Dream 144

The Teacher's Pet 147
Not Guilty 150
The Test of the Best 153
Part-Time Help 156
Forgotten 159
The Promotion 162
Planning Ahead 165
Dreams Come True 168
Caught! 172
The Checker Game 175
The Substitute 178
The Finished Product 181
God Provides 184
Grandparents Are Grand ... 187
The Stress Test 190
Trapped 193
A Safe Hiding Place 196
Right But Wrong 199
Pay Attention 202
Excuses, Excuses 205
Double Trouble 208
Which Is Greater? 211
Hard-Headed Howard ... 214
One More Night 217
A World of Difference ... 220
Sin's Chains 223
Warning! 226
Bugs in the Works 229
The Fire Escape 232
The Repellent 235
No Way Out 238
Pulling Up Roots 241
Oatmeal? Again? 244
Frozen Pipe 247
Behind the Scenes 250
Inside the Fence 253
Sharla's Idol 256
Following Instructions ... 260
Brother Trouble 263
One Step at a Time 266
The Second Chance 269
Keep Out 272
Out of Control 275
The Grumble Bug 278
Moving Day 281
Index 284

One-A-Day Pocket Stories

Just a minute.

Before you turn another page,
READ THIS.

Devotions can be an I-can-hardly-wait time of day. One-A-Day Pocket Stories will help you get excited about studying the Bible. Read it alone or with your family.
Here's how to use it.

1. *Riddle*

Some are tricky.
Some are sticky.
So don't be picky.
Just enjoy them all.

A riddle or question begins each devotional. The answers can be found in the Scripture or story. So keep reading.

2. *Key Verse*

A verse a day
Keeps the devil away.
Read it. Memorize it. Store it in your heart for the future.

The verses are quoted from the *New King James Version* of the Bible. It has the same meaning as the *King James Version*, but it uses modern English, which is easier to understand.

3. *Scripture Reading*

Read it carefully.
Read it prayerfully.

When you finish this book, you will have read all the major stories in Genesis through Deuteronomy. And you will have studied the first two thousand years of time.

Wow! That's a lot of days to cram into one book and one brain!

4. Story
Ever feel fear curl up your toes?
Ever hate your big, ugly nose?
Ever lose your best friend to another?
Ever fuss with your sister or brother?

Then you'll enjoy meeting the kids in these stories who are just like you.

5. The Reason
The Bible makes sense.
Read it with confidence.
Consider the evidence,
Or pay the consequence.

At the end of each story is a short paragraph connecting the Bible story with life today. Think or talk about the questions. They will help you relate God's Word to right here, right now.

6. The Rhyme
Then wrap up devotion time
With a simple little rhyme.

A Colorful Variety

God placed it everywhere,
Sea, earth, and sky.
It makes life beautiful.
What did God make and why?

___ ___ ___ ___ ___

Key Verse:
But if you show partiality, you commit sin (James 2:9).

Scripture Reading:
Genesis 1:1-13

"A boy just my age moved in next door," five-year-old Kevin announced.

Denise threw her notebook on the coffee table. "I hope they have a girl my age."

"They do." Kevin nibbled on an apple. "She's twelve, just like you, and her name is Jennifer. Michael doesn't have a bicycle or even a skateboard, but I told him not to worry, he could ride mine."

As Denise peeled an orange she said, "I guess I should go over and introduce myself."

Mrs. Wright smiled. "A good idea. You can take them a loaf of homemade bread."

Later as Denise stepped out the door carrying the warm bread, the door of the adjoining apartment opened. Denise gasped and tried not to stare.

The girl facing her smiled. "Hello. You must be Denise. I'm Jennifer. Your little brother has told my little brother all about you. I hope my little brother didn't tell your little brother too much about me," she laughed.

Denise tried to erase the surprise from her face. "No, he didn't tell me much at all." She thought, *He didn't tell me enough. Wait until I get my hands on that brat!*

"Won't you come in?" Jennifer invited.

"Ahhh . . . ahhh . . . no, thank you, not this time. My mother has dinner ready. She just sent me over with this bread." She thrust the bread into Jennifer's arms and fled.

As Denise entered the kitchen she snarled, "Why didn't you tell me, you little mutt?"

Kevin's eyes widened. "Tell you what?"

"Tell me about her . . . about them!" Denise ground her teeth.

Mrs. Wright took her place at the table. "What about them, Denise?"

Denise dropped into her chair. "What . . . what color. . . . "

"Oh, that," Kevin interrupted. "What difference does that make?"

"But they're the only people in this complex who are . . . who aren't like us," Denise argued.

Mrs. Wright shook her head. "No. Everyone in this complex is different. No two people are alike."

After saying grace, Mrs. Wright passed the food. "Look at the food, Denise. Isn't it pretty? Look at the green peas. . . ."

"Peas! Yuck!" Kevin interrupted.

Mrs. Wright continued, ". . . the deep red tomatoes, the yellow squash, the white potatoes. Vegetables are different colors, flowers are different colors. . . ."

"And people are different colors," Kevin added. "It makes the world beautiful. I think Michael's neat. I like white people." Kevin grinned, "Mom, if I clean up my plate, can I have a piece of chocolate cake?"

The Reason:
(Riddle answer: color)

God added beauty to His creation by giving us color and variety. Don't allow prejudices to keep you from making friends with someone simply because they are different. We are all different. Thank the Lord!
- Look around you. How many colors can you see?
- Close your eyes. Try to imagine what the world would look like without color.
- Make a new friend this week by reaching out to someone who is different.

Roses are red.
Violets are blue.
I'm glad I'm different,
And you are too.

2

In the Dark

Far, far away,
Never seen in a day;
The darker it is,
The better you see it.
What is it?

___ ___ ___ ___

Key Verse:
Though I walk in the midst of trouble, You will revive me (Psalm 138:7).

Scripture Reading:
Genesis 1:14-19

"Test tomorrow." Mr. Morgan's final words filled Trevor with dread.

"Brother!" he muttered. "Mr. Morgan's mind runs on one track, a test track."

After poring over his math book for an hour that evening, Trevor was in an even darker frame of mind. "It just doesn't make sense!" he exploded.

"What?" Mr. Webster shifted the little girl on his lap to a more comfortable position.

In the Dark

Trevor slammed his book shut. "Fractions! When Mr. Morgan starts talking fractions, the light goes out in my head."

Cindy peered at her big brother. "You got a light in your head, Trevor?"

Trevor snorted, "No. It's burned out."

Mr. Webster stood Cindy on her feet. "It's your bedtime, little girl. Go to your mother." She hobbled from the room.

Trevor watched with dark eyes. "Why does everything happen to us?" he asked for the hundredth time. "Cindy is born crippled, you lose your job, and I can't even pass a math test."

Mr. Webster stood up. "You haven't failed yet. Let me show you a few tricks."

Later Mrs. Webster came into the room and dropped into the recliner. "Finally, Cindy is asl. . . ."

"Mommy! Mommy!" Cindy's frightened wail brought them running. Mrs. Webster was the first to reach her bedside.

"I'm s-s-s-scared. It's dark in here," the little girl sobbed. "Turn on the light."

Mr. Webster and Trevor laughed as Mrs. Webster gently pulled the blanket from Cindy's face. "The night light is on, Cindy. You had your head covered."

Still chuckling, Trevor and his parents returned to the living room. "Sometimes we're like Cindy," Mr. Webster commented. "We have had some trouble. It's pretty dark, but the light is still on. We have much to be thankful for if we'll just uncover our heads."

Trevor sighed as he went back to his studies, "I'll be thankful if I pass that test." A little later, he looked up and grinned, "Finally, I'm seeing the light."

"Trevor," piped a little voice, "did the light come back on in your head?"

"Cindy!" Mother jumped up. "You get right back in bed." Taking her hand, Mrs. Webster walked her down the hall.

Mr. Webster winked at his son as they heard the little girl say, "But, Mother, I was just about to sleep when this light came on in my head and woke me up."

The Reason:
(Riddle answer: star)

When God created this world, He put lights in the night. In God's Word light represents understanding and hope. Just as there is day and night, life is made of trouble and blessings. The stars shine brightest when it is dark, and we can better count our blessings in the midst of trouble.
- Quit being afraid of what might happen.
- Look at the stars tonight. As you gaze at God's night lights, thank Him for the blessings He has given you.
- Hope in God. Things will be better tomorrow.

In the night,
God gives light.

The Creative Word 3

"Sticks and stones may break my bones, But words can never hurt me."

True or False?

Key Verse:

Let the words of my mouth and the meditation of my heart be acceptable in Your sight, O Lord (Psalm 19:14).

Scripture Reading:

Genesis 1:20-31

Giggles surrounded Heather. She turned to the five-year olds, her eyes blazing, "How many times do I have to tell you to stay out of my room?"

Silence stiffled the air. "B-B-But we were just p-p-passing through," Kendra sniffed.

"Yeah?" Heather curled her lip. "Get up and get out!"

Later as Heather entered the kitchen, Kevin was hopping around on one foot. "Grampa Harris is coming for dinner! I love for Grampa to come. He's so much fun."

Heather ignored him. "Mother, where is my new CD? If those brats have touched it, I'll. . . ."

Mrs. James held up her hand. "Enough, Heather! You'll find your new CD where you left it . . . in the CD player."

As she left the room, Heather heard Kevin grumble, "She spoils everything. We have fun until she comes home."

I spoil everything! What about them? Nobody around here understands. Nobody! With a sob, she ran to her room and slammed the door.

When Heather joined the family for dinner, Grampa was seated in the place of honor. No one commented on Heather's red, swollen face. It was a common sight.

During dinner, everyone, even Heather, laughed and talked and listened. "I'm glad you're here, Grampa," Heather commented. "You make us all feel so good."

Kevin took his last bite of lemon cake. "Yeah, even Heather laughs when you're here."

Mr. James gave the little boy a warning look as he pushed back his chair. "Let's go into the living room."

Grampa looked at his watch. "I'll have to leave soon. Let's read a few verses in the Bible and have prayer."

Kendra ran to get the large-print Bible. She leaned over the old man's shoulder and pointed, "Right there. See that little checkmark? That's where we stopped last night."

Grampa squinted. "Genesis chapter one and verse twenty." When he closed the Bible he said, "So we are made in God's image. That means we have His characteristics, His emotions and His abilities." He looked at Heather. "How did God create the world, Heather?"

Heather shrugged. "He just spoke and it happened."

Grampa nodded. "He created the world with His Word. He said, 'Let it be,' and it was. God has given us the ability to create some things with our words too."

Heather looked skeptical. "Now, Grampa. . . ."

"We can create happiness or gloom," Grampa continued. "Our words can build people up or tear them down. Our words can hurt or heal."

"You make happiness with your words," Kendra told the old gentleman.

"That's why we love for you to come," Kevin added.

And for once, Heather didn't say anything. She just listened . . . and thought, *That's why I've been so unhappy lately. I've created my own gloom cloud.*

The Reason:
(Riddle answer: false)

With His Word God created a beautiful world. With his word Satan tried to destroy it. Words are powerful, creative tools. Use them wisely.
- What kind of atmosphere do you create with your words?
- Do you build people up or tear them down?
- Think of a way you can build up someone in your family with your words.

Words are strong: use them right.
They make hearts heavy or make them light.

4

Only One Rule

You can't touch it, but you can feel it.
The more you give away
The more you have left.
What is it?

___ ___ ___ ___

Key Verse:
And this commandment we have from Him: that he who loves God must love his brother also (I John 4:21).

Scripture Reading:
Genesis 2:15-23; Mark 12:28-34

"Would you look at this list of rules?" Cindi dropped the paper on the kitchen bar. "The higher I go in school, the more rules I have to remember."

Mrs. English laughed. "And when you start driving, there will be even more."

Cindi grinned. "I won't mind those. Just three years, eleven months and . . . hummmmm . . . eleven days."

"Cindi! Cindi!" Four-year-old Brad jumped into the room. "Take me to the park, please?"

"After I eat a bite," she promised. As she ate she complained, "I'm getting fed up with rules. I thought when I got to be a teenager I'd have some freedom. Instead, there are more rules than ever!"

Mrs. English listened sympathetically. "I understand how you feel, but there is a reason for every rule."

Cindi grimaced. "I know. I've heard that before. But, Mother, it's been so long since you were a teenager, you've forgotten what. . . ."

"Hurry up," Brad pulled at her sleeve. "Let's go."

Cindi stood up. "Alright. Let me get my books. I'll study while you play. That's the reward of growing up."

At the park Cindi settled down on a bench. "Only one rule for you, little boy," she said. "Don't go near the duck pond."

Brad nodded and ran for a swing. Cindi settled down to study. Several minutes later she looked up. "Brad? Brad? Bradley Duane English?" No little boy and no answer. She jumped to her feet. *Where could he be?* Cindi knew immediately. *The duck pond.*

As she pulled a wet and muddy little boy home, she scolded, "You could have gone anywhere in the park but the duck pond. So where did you go? The duck pond."

Later as Brad soaked in the bathtub, Cindi said to her mother, "He only had one rule to obey, and he broke it."

Mrs. English smiled. "Adam and Eve had only one rule."

"I wish that was all I had," Cindi replied.

"Really it is," Mrs. English answered. "There is one law that covers all the rest."

Cindi wrinkled her brow. "What?"

"The law of love," Mrs. English explained. "If we love God and love one another, it is easy to obey the other laws."

"I'm not so sure. . . ." Cindi began.
"Mommy, I'm ready to get out," Brad called.
Over her shoulder Mrs. English said, "Think about it."

The Reason:
(Riddle answer: love)

If everyone loved one another as they should, there would be no theft, no murder, and no violence. Most laws and rules would not be needed if we truly loved God and one another. Let love be the ruling force in your life, and you will not have to worry about breaking man's laws.
- What *rule* in your family do you have the most trouble obeying?
- What is the reason for that rule?
- How could love make it easier for you to obey it?

At home, at church, at school,
Make love the golden rule.

The First Mistake

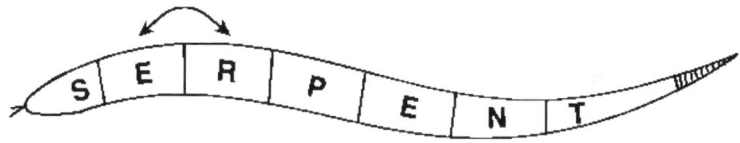

Delete the "s" in serpent.
Rearrange the other letters.
When you sin, do this,
And you'll sure feel better.

___ ___ ___ ___ ___ ___

Key verse:
  Flee also youthful lusts (II Timothy 2:22).

Scripture Reading:
  Genesis 3:1-13

"Please, Andrea, I need a cupcake sooooo bad!" four-year-old Sara pleaded.

Andrea almost weakened but she shook her head. "Sorry. I just have twenty-eight, exactly enough for my class party tomorrow. Now run and play." Andrea ordered her little sister as she took the last cupcakes out of the oven.

A stubborn look covered Sara's face. "I wanna watch."

Andrea sighed, "OK. But it'll just make you hungrier."

As Andrea was frosting the last cupcake, the living room phone rang. Fifteen minutes later she was telling Monica good-bye when Mrs. Walker came home.

"Yummmm. Sure smells good in here." Mrs. Walker deposited the grocery sacks on the cabinet. "Your cupcakes look delicious, Andrea. I'll bring them to school for you. You'll never be able to carry them on the bus."

"You won't need to bother, Mother," Andrea answered breezily. "Monica volunteered to give me . . . a ride . . . to. . . ."

Mrs. Walker stood still. "Andrea, you know how we feel about your friendship with Monica. Furthermore, you are not to ride anywhere with that boy she is dating."

Andrea glared, "I'm old enough to choose my own friends."

Mrs. Walker sighed. "Then prove it. Tim Blankenship was arrested last week for DWI, and Monica. . . ."

"Monica's okay," Andrea argued. "She's just different."

Mrs. Walker looked sad. "And you're different, too, since you started running around with her."

"Don't you trust me?" Andrea raged. "I'm a Christian. I know right from wrong."

"Being a Christian won't change things one bit if you're a passenger in a car driven by a drunk," Mrs. Walker responded. "Christians die young, too, you know."

"Ooohhhh!" Andrea sputtered.

Mrs. Walker started putting up the groceries. "You are not riding anywhere with Monica and Tim."

Angry tears poured down Andrea's cheeks as she arranged the cupcakes on a tray. "Twenty-six . . . twenty seven," she counted. She stopped and counted again. "Sara? Sara!" The little girl was gone.

Andrea found her in the bathroom washing the frosting off her face. "I ought to shake you." She ground her teeth.

Sara's eyes widened. "But, Andrea, your cupcakes smelled soooo good and looked soooo good, and my tummy just kept begging for one."

"Your first mistake was not leaving the kitchen; then you wouldn't have been tempted," Andrea snapped.

"You're right." Andrea jumped as Mrs. Walker spoke behind her. "Rule one to overcoming sin is stay away from it! And that's why...."

"I know! I know!" Andrea took a deep breath. "That's why I shouldn't hang around with Monica and her crowd. Oooohhhh, why do you always have to be right?"

'Cause ... she's ... the ... mother, ... that's ... why," Sara answered simply. Then she smiled sweetly at her big sister. "Don't be mad, Andrea. I just ate your cupcake. You've still got enough for everyone else."

The Reason:
(Riddle answer: repent)

Eve's first mistake was staying around the tree of the knowledge of good and evil. You won't be tempted to read dirty magazines unless you stand around the magazine rack and read the covers. If something is wrong, stay away from it. You're a lot safer that way.

- What are some sins we should stay away from?
- Do you have friends who pressure you to go places and do things you shouldn't?
- Make a list of people and places that you will avoid.

Stay away from sin
And it won't get in.

6

Side Effects

Eve was guilty, and Adam too.
But don't get proud. So are you.
A three-letter word will solve this riddle.
Need a clue?" "I" am in the middle.
  ___ I ___

Key Verse:
Through one man sin entered the world, and death through sin (Romans 5:12).

Scripture Reading:
Genesis 3:14-24

"Jason, dinner is ready. And don't forget to put up your skateboard!" Mrs. Nelson called out the front door.

"Nag! Nag!" Jason muttered as he kicked the skateboard to one side of the driveway. "I've been told that a hundred times. You'd think I was a baby."

In the kitchen he took one look at his little sister and burst out laughing. Her face was covered with bright red splotches. "Boy, you look funny."

"I don't feel funny," Amy snapped. "I itch all over."

"Amy is having a reaction to the shot the doctor gave her. He warned us there might be side effects."

"I'd call it face effects," Jason chuckled.

"I've got splotches on my side, too," the little girl announced. "I have them all over me."

After Mr. Nelson offered grace he asked, "Did you hear about the accident on Turner Road?"

"No." Mrs. Nelson passed the fried chicken. "What happened?"

Mr. Nelson looked very angry. "Somebody stole a stop sign, probably wanted a souvenir. A van filled with children and a dump truck collided at the intersection."

Mrs. Nelson gasped. Jason asked, "Was anyone killed?"

Mr. Nelson nodded. "Yes, two little boys. Several people are in critical condition."

Mrs. Nelson's face tightened. "I hope that thief spends many sleepless nights."

Amy wiggled. "I itch," she complained.

Mr. Nelson looked thoughtful. "Sin has side effects, too. Because someone stole that stop sign, many people are hurting tonight."

Mrs. Nelson nodded. "When we sin we not only hurt ourselves, but we hurt others too."

A big knot rose in Jason's throat as he thought about the little boys who had died in the wreck.

At bedtime, Mrs. Nelson went out to call in the dog. "Here, Frisk . . . ooooohhh!" she screamed.

Jason was the first to reach her. "Daddy! Daddy! Come quick! Mother's hurt."

Mrs. Nelson rose up on one elbow and fell back with a groan. "Ohhhh, my back! What happened?"

Mr. Nelson knelt beside her. "You tripped on Jason's skateboard."

Tears rolled down Jason's cheeks. "I'm sorry, Mother. I'm sorry. I meant to put it up later."

Several hours later Mr. Nelson sat on the edge of Jason's bed. "I'm so s-s-sorry," the boy sobbed. "How long will Mother have to be in the h-h-hospital?"

"Several days." Mr. Nelson put his arm around the boy. "You are forgiven. But it's like we said at dinner; our actions have side effects. Now let's talk to The Lord."

As they knelt, Mr. Nelson felt a soft little hand slip into his. "Side effects aren't funny," whispered Amy as she scratched her neck.

The Reason:
(Riddle answer: sin)

We are still suffering the side effects of Adam and Eve's sin . . . weeds, pain, and hard work. The next time you are tempted to sin, remember: sin always produces side effects.
- What changed when Adam and Eve sinned?
- What would life be like today if they had not sinned?
- How can one family member's sin affect the rest of the family?

Sin always hurts another;
Don't forget it, brother.

7

The Emergency Brake

The more you lose it,
The more you have it.
What is it?

___ ___ ___ ___ ___ ___

Key Verse:
Whoever hates his brother is a murderer (I John 3:15).

Scripture Reading:
Genesis 4:1-8

"Wally never does anything wrong! It's always me! Sometimes I hate him!" Marla screamed as she ran from the room, slamming the door behind her.

With a heavy frown, Mrs. Austin started after her daughter. But honking horns changed her direction. She ran out onto the porch and almost collided with Wally. Over his shoulder she saw a car careening down the hill. Wally yelled above the confusion, "Look, Mom! Mrs. Parker's car's out of control. She left it running while she went in the house. Guess she forgot to pull the emergency brake. Look at that car go!"

Marla carne running out of the house. "What's happening?"

Wally pointed at the runaway car, while Mrs. Austin prayed, "Please, Lord, stop it before it gets to the intersection."

At that moment the car turned sharply, jumped the curb, and ran into a tree. "Thank God!" the trio on the porch gasped.

When the excitement was over, Wally returned to his yard work. Marla picked up the evening paper and followed her mother into the kitchen.

"I need a current event for social studies." She sat down at the table. She flipped the pages of the paper. "Here's one. 'Woman Shoots Neighbor in Jealous Rage.' Boy, people are awful."

"Yes," Mrs. Austin agreed. "Most fits of anger are awful . . . and dangerous. An uncontrolled temper is like a runaway car. No doubt, that woman's problem started when she was a jealous little girl who slammed doors and threw temper tantrums."

Marla frowned. "Just because I slammed a door doesn't mean I'm going to commit murder."

Mrs. Austin sat down at the table. "Just because a car careens down a street out of control doesn't mean it will kill anyone either. But it could. It's a dangerous situation, and I intend for you to learn now how to control your temper, Marla. If you don't put on the brakes, I'll do it for you."

Marla didn't want to grin, but she couldn't help it. "OK, Mother. I get the point. Next time I feel a temper tantrum coming on, I'll pull the emergency brake."

The Reason:
(Riddle answer: temper)

When Abel's sacrifice was accepted by God and Cain's was rejected, Cain became "very wroth." He lost control! When your temper gets bigger than you are, you've got trouble. Put the brakes on your temper or it will push you to do something you will forever regret.

- Why was Cain jealous of Abel? How can jealousy lead to murder?
- Is it ever okay to get angry?
- What are some ways you can control your temper?

Put on the brakes,
That's all it takes.

8

The All-Seeing Eye

What did Cain say to Adam before he killed him?

Key Verse:
The eyes of the L ORD are in every place, keeping watch on the evil and the good (Proverbs 15:3).

Scripture Reading:
Genesis 4:9-16

Shanna switched on the bedside lamp, rolled her eyes at the closed door, and pulled a magazine from under her mattress. She snuggled deeply into the cover and flipped the pages. Her face burned, and her heart thumped.

You shouldn't . . . , her conscience began.

"Awwww, hush up!" Shanna's mind ordered. *I'm not a baby anymore. I'm almost a teenager. There are some things I need to know.*

God ssees. . . her conscience began.

Knock-knock. Quickly, Shanna hid the magazine. "May I come in, honey?" Mrs. Bryant opened the door.

"S-S-S-Sure. Sure, come in," Shanna invited.

Her mother sat down on the edge of the bed. "I wondered if you had time to go with Michael and me to visit Aunt Sadie tomorrow. She would love to see you."

"I guess I could," Shanna replied in her martyr voice.

Mrs. Bryant kissed her daughter good night. "Great. Now get a good night's sleep." She switched off the lamp as she left, closing the door behind her.

The magazine poked Shanna's leg. She wanted to read some more but dared not turn the light on. So she stuffed the magazine under the mattress and fluffed her pillow. It was a long time before she went to sleep.

Returning from Aunt Sadie's the next afternoon, Shanna remarked, "What a deserted stretch of road." Six-year-old Michael leaned over the front seat.

"Shanna, does God see everything we do?"

Shanna's eyebrows went up. What would this kid ask next? "I guess so. Why?"

"I just wondered," Michael shrugged. "I saw Justin looking at some dirty pictures. Should I tell his mother or let God?"

Shanna's face burned. She stared out the side window. Surely that brat hadn't been snooping in her room!

Mrs. Bryant answered, "I think you'd better let God."

"OK." Michael looked over his shoulder. "Did you know there's a patrolman behind us? Are you speeding, Mom?"

"I certainly hope not." Mrs. Bryant glanced at the speedometer. "No, I'm all right."

For several miles the patrolman followed them. "I wish he'd pass," Shanna fussed. "He's making me nervous."

Mother grinned. "Relax, honey. I'm obeying the law."

Thump! Thump! Thump! Mrs. Bryant pulled at the steering wheel.

"What's the matter, Mom?" Shanna asked as her mother pulled the car off the highway.

"I think we have a flat!" Mrs. Bryant groaned. "And I've never in my whole life changed a tire. What will. . . ."

"Need some help, ma'am?" asked a gruff voice. Mrs. Bryant jumped. The patrolman stood beside the window.

Mrs. Bryant smiled, "Oh, I'm so glad to see you."

After the patrolman changed the tire he said, "I'll follow you to a station, ma'am."

As they pulled back onto the highway, Shanna sighed, "How nice. Makes me feel good to know he's behind us."

Mrs. Bryant smiled, "Yes. How we feel about being watched depends upon what we are doing."

Shanna nodded as she told herself, *When you get home, gal, there's something under your mattress that has got to go!*

The Reason:

(Riddle answer: Cain didn't kill Adam; he killed Abel.)

Cain thought he could cover his sin, but he couldn't. God does not watch us so He can catch us, but so He can protect us. Knowing God is watching is a comforting thought when you are obeying His laws.

- How does it make you feel to know God is watching you . . . nervous or comfortable?
- Is there sin in your life? If so, now is the time to get rid of it.
- Say a prayer of thanksgiving to God for watching over you.

Whether you're wrong or right,
You're always in God's sight.

9

Best Friends

For 365 days a year for 365 years,
I walked with God.
Who am I?

Key Verse:
Can two walk together, unless they are agreed? (Amos 3:3).

Scripture Reading:
Genesis 5:21-27

"I'll" have to ask. Yeah, got ya. See ya tomorrow." Mark hung up the phone. He turned to face his mother. "Jason wants to know . . . uhhhh . . . if 1 can go with some of the fellows to the mall . . . uhhhh . . . tomorrow night."

Mrs. Clark put down her book. "Tomorrow night? That's Bible study, Mark."

Anger darkened Mark's eyes. "I know, but Bible study's for adults. It wouldn't hurt for me to miss once."

His mother shook her head. "Since you've started running around with Jason, your attitude has changed

. . . and not for the better. I'm really concerned about your walk with God."

"I'm old enough to choose my friends," Mark growled. "I don't need to go to church all the time. I've got other. . . ."

"I've got a new friend," sang six-year-old Cindi as she danced into the room. "Her name is Becky and we're going to walk home from school together every day. You don't have to wait on me anymore, Mark. I'm going to walk with my new friend."

"That suits me just fine!" Mark stomped from the room.

The next day after school, Mark waited for Cindi at the usual corner. But she waved gaily as she ran past, hand-in-hand with a little girl her size. "I don't need you, Mark. I'm walking with Becky."

Mark hesitated. He wouldn't admit it, but he was a little hurt that Cindi had dismissed him so cheerfully. "I'd better keep her in sight," he muttered. "Don't want anything to happen to her." So he tagged along behind the giggling, skipping girls.

Mother met them at the door with her purse in hand. "Grandfather Clark just had a heart attack. We've got to go to the hospital."

As they sped down the freeway, Mark prayed for the first time in a long time, "O, Lord, we need You. Please. . . ."

At the hospital, Mrs. Clark deposited the children in the waiting room and disappeared down the hall. Much later she returned. "Granddad is asking for you, Mark. Come with me."

Fear clutched Mark's heart as he entered a small cubicle filled with machines and tubes and nurses. Granddad lay on a high bed. As Mark approached, he opened his eyes and smiled weakly. "Hi, Son. Just wanted to tell you not to worry about me. I've been walking with the Lord for a long time, and I'm ready to go wherever He leads me." Granddad paused to catch his breath. "Just keep living for God and walking with Him. Then you won't ever have to be afraid of anything . . . not even death." Granddad closed his eyes and the nurse motioned for Mark to leave.

As he walked down the hospital hall, Mark thought about Granddad walking with God, and Cindi walking with Becky, and him walking with Jason. He leaned against the wall and closed his eyes. Two tears rolled down his cheeks. "God," he whispered, "could I walk with You again? I'm sorry I acted like I didn't need You." He took a deep breath. "And, God, if You want to take Granddad home with You, I guess that's okay, too. After all, You're his best friend."

The Reason:
(Riddle answer: Enoch)

To walk with God means to go where He wants you to go, and to do what He wants you to do. For 365 years Enoch and God walked together. They were best friends and agreed about everything. Then one day Enoch went home with God. When you walk with God, you don't have to be afraid of anything . . . not even death.
- How do we walk and talk with God?
- Where are some places you cannot go if you walk with God?
- How can walking with God take away your fear of death?

With God agree,
From fear be free.

10

It's OK to Be Different

What animal brought his luggage onto the ark?

Key Verse:
But you are a chosen generation, a royal priesthood, a holy nation, His own special people (I Peter 2:9).

Scripture Reading:
Genesis 6:1-8

Lisa flung herself down on the sofa and soaked a pillow with her tears. Hearing her sobs, Mr. Wright came into the living room and dropped down beside her. "Baby, whatever is the matter?"

Lisa choked down a sob and turned her swollen face toward her father. "I'm s-s-s-sick of being different," she blurted out. "I'm the only girl in my c-c-class who doesn't wear jeans, and doesn't cut her hair, and doesn't go to the movies, and doesn't. . . ." she gulped for air. "Oh, Daddy, why can't I be like everybody else?"

Mr. Wright pushed Lisa's hair out of her face. "You're also the only girl in your class who has the baptism of the Holy Ghost," he reminded. "You're one of the few who lives with both parents and never has to worry about her dad coming home drunk or her mother filing for a divorce or. . . ."

"Oooohhhh," Lisa's sobs increased. "You're making me feel so ashamed." She sat up quickly. "Either I'm ashamed for being different or I'm ashamed for being ashamed."

Mr. Wright stood up and pulled her to her feet. "I'm going up in the mountains on business. Go with me."

Lisa nodded. "Wait till I blow my nose and wash my face."

The crisp fall mountain air quickly cheered her. "I love the mountains," she sighed. "They're so . . . so awesome."

"I'm always impressed by the greatness of God when I see His handiwork," Mr. Wright said. "How big God is!" Lisa leaned closer to the windshield and peered up, up, up, but she couldn't see the top of the mountain in front of them. "Look, Dad. Look at that crimson tree up there." Mr. Wright glanced up the mountainside. Lisa continued, "It sure stands out . . . the only red tree in the middle of a thousand green ones. It's beautiful!"

Mr. Wright nodded, "Yes, honey. That must be how you look to God, the only Christian in your class."

Lisa's eyes widened as she stared at the red tree. "Then it's okay to be different. I wouldn't want to be any other way."

The Reason:

(Riddle answer: The elephant—he brought his trunk.)

The world was so wicked that God was sorry He had made man. So, He decided to give His creation a bath. But then He saw someone who was different. Noah, a righteous man, stood out in a world filled with violence and wickedness. He got God's attention. It's okay to be different. God is looking for righteous people who stand out. Do you stand out?

- In what ways are you glad to be different from the world?
- In what ways would you like to be "like everybody else"?
- How do you think God feels about the way you look and act?

To be different is okay;
God likes His kids to be that way.

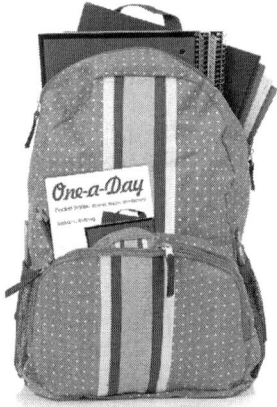

Get In

What was the favorite fruit in the ark?

Key Verse:
And as it was in the days of Noah, so it will be also in the days of the Son of Man (Luke 17:26).

Scripture Reading:
Genesis 6:9-14; 7:11-17

As the evangelist pleaded, Mother put her arm around Trena's shoulders. She whispered, "Honey, when are you going to get in the church?"

Trena snapped back, "Where do you think I am?"

Mother shook her head. Softly she said, "You're in the church building, but you are not in the church, Trena."

Trena knew what Mother meant. She was twelve years old and had not repented, nor been baptized in Jesus' name, nor received the Holy Ghost. She knew she was not in the church. She also knew she was tired of people pressuring her to get in.

When Mother saw the stubborn look on Trena's face, she dropped her arm and joined the others going to pray. Trena sat down on the pew alone to wait.

When she came in from school the next day, Trena was surprised to see a backhoe digging a large hole in their yard. "What are they doing, Mother?" she asked.

"Building a storm cellar," Mrs. Cook replied.

"But they're messing up the lawn and your flower bed."

"I know, but we need a storm cellar."

"How much will it cost?" Trena asked.

Mrs. Cook grimaced, "A couple thousand dollars." Trena whistled. "That's a lot of money!"

"I know." Mrs. Cook dried her hands on a tea towel. "But just one tornado would make it worth every penny."

Weeks passed. The cellar was finished. Trena went to church every service, but she refused to get in.

One evening as the Cooks sat down to dinner, Mother remarked, "It sure looks stormy."

Mr. Cook nodded. "There are storm warnings out for. . . ." Suddenly the shriek of the storm siren startled them. They jumped to their feet.

"I'll get the portable radio and flashlight," Mr. Cook said. "Get Tippy, Trena. We're going to the cellar."

Large drops of rain pelted them as they pushed against the wind crossing the lawn. Just as Trena started down the cellar steps, Tippy wiggled from her arms and ran excitedly toward the house.

"Tippy! Tippy! Come back!" Trena screamed frantically. "Daddy, get Tippy!"

The rain changed to hail. The wind screeched through the trees. "Get in the cellar, Trena," Mr. Cook ordered. "I'll get him."

Trena hesitated until Mrs. Cook pulled her inside. They spent a few tense seconds before Mr. Cook came panting down the steps carrying a dripping puppy.

"You silly little puppy!" Trena scolded. "Don't you have sense enough to get in the cellar when a storm is coming?"

Mrs. Cook looked straight at her daughter. "What about you, Trena? Don't you have sense enough to get in the church when the Rapture is coming?"

Trena's heart did a double flip. "I-I-I wish there was an altar in this cellar. I'm ready to get in."

Mr. Cook beamed. "We can make an altar anywhere, any time. Let's pray."

The Reason:
(Riddle answer: pear/pair)

Just as God provided Noah a way of escape from the flood, He has provided us a way of escape from the judgment coming upon this earth. The church is our ark. But to be saved, we must get in.

- Have you obeyed Acts 2:38—repented of your sins, been baptized in Jesus' name, and received the Holy Ghost?
- Are you playing around, in and out of the church? Don't do it. It's dangerous.
- Are you ready for the Rapture? If not, now is the time to get ready.

Don't wait too late!

12

Not Forgotten

What can God not forget?

Key Verse:
See, I have inscribed you on the palms of My hands (Isaiah 49:16).

Scripture Reading:
Genesis 8:1-19

Steven blew his mother a kiss and jumped from the car. "No, you don't need to come with me. I'm in the third grade, remember," he said firmly.

Mrs. Johnson asked, "Are you sure you know where your room is?"

Steven snorted, "Of course." The day before she had enrolled him in his new school. He had visited his room and met his teacher.

"Your dad will pick you up after school," Mrs. Johnson reminded. "Wait for him in the hall outside your room."

With his head high, Steven marched across the playground. His heart was thump-thumping, but no one knew that. All he needed was a friend, and he'd told

God about that last night so he wasn't worried . . . well, not too worried, just a little lonely.

All day Steven waited for his new friend to walk up and say, "Hi, I'm your new friend. Come play with me." But everyone just ignored him.

By the time the last bell rang, Steven was about to burst into tears. He stood in the hall, waiting for his dad and watching laughing, talking kids push past him. No one even said, "Excuse me."

Soon the halls were empty. Only the faint chatter of teachers visiting in the office drifted down the corridor. Where was his dad? Angrily, Steven brushed two tears from his cheeks and sniffed loudly. He felt so very, very lonely. God had forgotten to send him a new friend, and now his dad had forgotten to pick him up.

Straight across in front of him was a large photo of the kindest looking man Steven had ever seen. He walked across to look closer. An engraved plaque was attached to the bottom of the frame. Steven read softly, "Tom Carter, custodian." He wrinkled his brow. What was a custodian?

"That's my Uncle Tom," a voice beside him announced. Steven jumped. "Ha! Scared you didn't I? You thought everyone had gone home."

Steven recognized a boy from his class. "I'm waiting on my mom. She teaches fourth grade," the boy continued. "Uncle Tom used to be the custodian here."

"What's a custodian?" Steven asked.

The boy snorted, "A janitor. Uncle Tom was the best custodian this school ever had. He was the custodian for thirty-eight years. Mr. Winters, the principal, had this picture put up and his name engraved or inscribed on it so we would never forget him. He died last winter." He hesitated, and then as if he had made up his mind about something, he continued, "My name's Ben. How'd you like to be part of my science team?"

Steven's eyes brightened. "Sure, I. . . ."

"There you are, Steven." Mr. Johnson was coming down the hall with an embarrassed grin. "Would you believe I got lost in this building?"

Ben and Steven giggled. "That's all right, Dad. I was visiting with my new friend Ben . . . and his Uncle Tom."

The Reason:
(Riddle answer: you.)

Noah and his family spent one year and ten days in the ark! But God had not forgotten them. And God remembers us, too. We are engraved or inscribed on the palm of His hands. Look at your palms. If something was written there, you would see it constantly. So, we are constantly before the Lord. He never forgets us. And don't you forget it.

- What could happen if God forgot about this earth for one minute? Use your imagination.
- What is the most important thing you ever forgot?
- Have you ever felt as if God had forgotten you? Why? Had He?

Don't worry! Don't fret.
God has never forgotten us yet.

The Contract

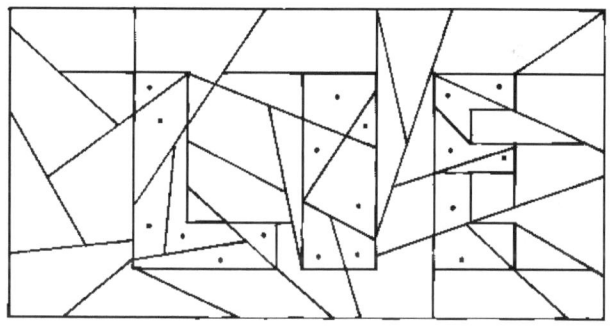

Fill in each area containing a dot to find what God cannot do.

Key Verse:
There has not failed one word of all His good promise (I Kings 8:56).

Scripture Reading:
Genesis 8:20-22; 9:8-17

"Whoopeeee!" Darren turned a somersault on the carpet. "We're going to get a new car. When, Dad? Tonight?"

Mr. Marlar laughed. "Slow down, Son. First, I have to go to the bank and get the money."

Darren puckered his lips. "How long will that take?"

"That depends. If it rains tomorrow and I don't have to work, we should have our car by evening."

"Could I go with you? Please, Dad?" Darren begged.

Mr. Marlar grinned, "If your mother doesn't object."

The next morning Darren jumped out of bed and ran to the window. He sang, "It's raining. It's raining."

Later, he sat excitedly beside his father, as Mr. Stevens, the banker, pushed a piece of paper across the desk. "Sign here, Mr. Marlar . . . and here . . . and here."

Darren's eyes widened as he looked at the long sheet covered with fine print that his father was signing.

When Mr. Marlar finished, Mr. Stevens stood up with a smile. As the men shook hands, the banker said, "We'll put the money in your account, Mr. Marlar." He extended his hand to Darren. "Enjoy that new car, Son."

Darren straightened his shoulders, shook the banker's hand, and replied, "Yes, sir. I will, sir. And . . . and . . . uhhhh thank you, sir."

Mr. Stevens chuckled, "You are most welcome. Anytime."

As they drove home in the new car, Mr. Marlar turned on the time-controlled wipers.

Darren peered at the black sky. "I hope it doesn't hail on our new car," he worried.

"I think the rain is about over," Mr. Marlar replied.

Darren fiddled with the radio buttons searching for a weather station. "What was that you signed at the bank?"

"A contract," Mr. Marlar answered.

Darren wrinkled his nose. "What's a contract?"

Mr. Marlar set the cruise control and leaned back. "It is an agreement between two people."

The Contract

"What did your contract with Mr. Stevens say?" Darren asked.

"It said a lot of things," Mr. Marlar began. Darren nodded, remembering all the fine print on the long paper. "But the bottom line was that the bank would loan me the money to buy this car if I agreed to pay it back in monthly payments for the next four years."

Darren whistled. "Four years? That's a long time. I'll be thirteen by then."

At that moment the sun slipped from under a cover of clouds. "Look!" Darren pointed toward the east. "Look, Dad, there's a rainbow. It's beautiful."

Mr. Marlar smiled. "Yes, it is. It's God's signature on a contract He made thousands of years ago with Noah. And, Son, remember this; just as I plan to keep my word and make the payments on this car, so God always keeps His Word."

The Reason:

(Riddle answer: lie. See Titus 1:2.)

God's Word is a covenant or a contract between God and man. The rainbow is God's "token" or signature on the contract that He would never again destroy the earth with a flood. Every time you see a rainbow, give thanks because God always keeps His Word.

- Think of an agreement you made with someone this week (such as, "I'll wash the dishes for you if you'll take me to the mall").
- What covenant did God make with Noah?
- How can you know that God will keep His Word?

A rainbow in the sky
Reminds us God cannot lie.

14

The Control Tower

Find the words in the box to fill in the blanks.

The Lord wanted the people to

_ _ _ _ _ _ _

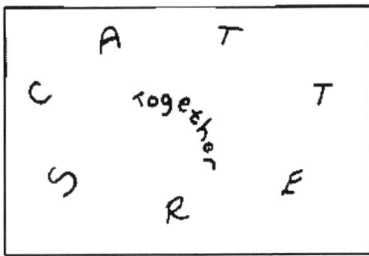

But they wanted to stick

_ _ _ _ _ _ _

Key Verse:
Out of heaven He let you hear His voice, that He might instruct you (Deuteronomy 4:36).

Scripture Reading:
Genesis 11:1-9

Nanci had a boyfriend! Of course, her mother and father believed twelve was too young. But she wasn't really dating Brad. He just carried her books home from school every day and bought her a Coke when he got his allowance. And, of course, her mother and father thought she shouldn't have a boyfriend who wasn't saved.

The Control Tower

"It's as if you don't trust me," she had argued.

"How about you trusting us to know what is best for you?" Mr. Maxwell had answered.

But Nanci wasn't thinking about Brad right now. She was taking her first plane ride in Uncle Leroy's twin engine. "Look down there, Mom!" Nanci yelled above the engine noise. "There's the tower. Everything looks so small."

Mother nodded, "I wonder if maybe that's how God sees things. What seems so big and important to us...."

"And look, Mom," Nanci interrupted. "Isn't that the mall? It looks like a little box." She chattered on and on, but the adults hardly heard. They were trying to visit.

Mrs. Maxwell leaned toward her brother at the controls. "How are you feeling, Leroy? You look a little worn."

"Thanks. Just what I would expect from a nurse," Uncle Leroy laughed. "I'm okay. Just a little tired."

The time passed so quickly that Nanci was surprised to hear her uncle getting clearance for their landing. "We're at...." he began. "Ohhhh! My chest...." He slumped forward.

"Leroy! What's wrong?" Mrs. Maxwell cried as she unfastened her seat belt and knelt beside him. His face was ashen and he did not answer. Mr. Maxwell pulled him from the pilot's seat. Then Mrs. Maxwell began giving him CPR.

"Oh, what's going to happen to us?" Nanci wailed. "Daddy can't fly this plane."

"Be calm and pray, Nanci." Mr. Maxwell glanced briefly at her. "The control tower will give us directions."

The next fifteen minutes were the longest of Nanci's life. She prayed for her mother and Uncle Leroy. She prayed for her father as he did his best to follow the step-by-step instructions from the control tower. And she prayed for herself. She didn't feel comfortable about dying. She thought about Brad and prayed harder.

The wheels bounced on the runway and the plane skidded to a stop. They took a deep breath. "Thank you, Jesus."

An ambulance was waiting. As Nanci's shaky legs carried her into the airport, she heard her father say, "Thank God for the control tower."

Later that night Mrs. Maxwell came into Nanci's room. "Uncle Leroy is going to make it," she reported. She turned to leave, but Nanci grabbed her hand.

"Mom, I'm sorry I've made such a big issue out of dating Brad. Up there in the plane, I realized having a boyfriend is not important, at least, not now. What's really important is that I follow the instructions I get from my control tower. And that's you and Daddy."

The Reason:
(Riddle answer: scatter, together)

Noah's growing family decided to stick together, instead of following their instructions from heaven's control tower to spread out. They didn't trust God to take care of them. They did it their way and got in trouble. God has given you parents and a pastor to guide your ways. Trust and obey them for a happy landing!

- Why do you think the people refused to spread out as God commanded?
- What would have happened if Mr. Maxwell had refused to obey the instructions from the control tower?
- Why has God instructed Christians not to date and marry unbelievers?

Obey. Don't pout.
Over and out.

15

Flying in the Fog

How much candy did the little boy want?
(Clue: What was the name of Abram's nephew?)
A ___ ___ ___.

Key Verse:
For we walk by faith, not by sight (II Corinthians 5:7).

Scripture Reading:
Genesis 12:1-9

But we can't move!" Zac cried. "All my friends are here."

Mrs. Michaels smiled gently. "I know, Son, but God is calling your father to start a church in Middlebrook."

"I won't have any friends at school or church or anywhere!" Zac wailed. "I don't want to move!"

Mr. Michaels put his hand on Zac's shoulder. "Son, we know it won't be easy, but. . . ."

Rrrrinnnggg. He dropped his hand. "I'll get it."

When he hung up the receiver, Mr. Michaels turned to his family. "My brother Bob has been injured in a car wreck. They are transferring him to the University Hospital in the city. He's calling for me. I've got to go."

Mrs. Michaels put her arm around her husband. "But, John, it will be morning before you can get there."

"Perhaps Roger Fields can fly me." Mr. Michaels went back to the phone. When he returned, he said, "It's all set. We leave in one hour. There's room for you and Zac, Martha, if you want to go."

Mrs. Michaels nodded. "Let's go pack."

As they drove to the airport, she worried. "How can we fly in this dense fog?"

"It's only ground fog," Mr. Michaels answered. "As soon as we get above it, we'll be all right."

Mr. Fields was waiting for them. He smiled at Zac. "Would you like to ride in the front with me?" Zac grinned and accepted the invitation.

Soon they were taxiing through the soupy fog down the runway. As they rose into the air, Zac felt like he had been enveloped in a dark gray comforter. "How can you tell which way to go, Mr. Fields?" he shouted.

Mr. Fields pointed at the cockpit control board. "By using the instruments. If I followed my own intuition, we probably would go in the opposite direction and land in Chicago," he laughed. "I argued with the instruments once. I was going to Dallas. I ended up in St. Louis. That was the first and last time I argued with them."

In a few minutes they lifted above the fog. A full moon surrounded by twinkling stars welcomed them. "Oh, it's beautiful," Zac whispered in awe.

The ride was over too soon for him.

As they sped toward the hospital in a rented car, Mrs. Michaels sighed, "I'm glad to be on solid ground. The fog and darkness made me nervous."

Zac turned to her in surprise. "I don't know why. Mr. Fields knew what he was doing. He's rated to fly with instruments, you know."

Mr. Michaels nodded. "Right. Roger's a good pilot. I wasn't worried. And I'm not worried about moving to Middlebrook either. The future may seem foggy and dark. Certainly, we have no way of knowing what will happen. But I trust God. He's at the controls."

Zac leaned back. "Hummmmmmm," he said. "Hummm. . . ."

The Reason:
(Riddle answer: lot)

When Abram left Haran, he didn't know where he was going, but he knew who was leading the way. He walked by faith, trusting God to show him each step.
- How do you think Sarah felt about leaving her home and friends?
- What advice would you give Zac to help him adjust to his new home in Middlebrook?
- Has your family ever moved from one city to another because "God wanted you to"?
- Make a list of the good things that have happened because your family obeyed God.

When God leads the way,
You cannot go astray.

16

The Cookie Jar

How do we know Abram made a passing grade in math?

Key Verse:
Give, and it will be given to you (Luke 6:38).

Scripture Reading:
Genesis 13:2-17

Amy and Nick were playing in the back yard with their cousin Jake when Mrs. Boyd came out the back door. "Here are some chocolate chip cookies, kids," she called as she sat a sack on the picnic table.

The children came running. "Yummmmmm, I love chocolate chip cookies." Jake rubbed his stomach. "How many are there'!?"

Amy counted. "Six. Two each."

"I'll take mine right now." Jake grabbed for the sack.

As he did, it fell onto the patio, crumbling the cookies.

"Now look what you've done!" Amy scolded as she hurriedly reached for the sack. But Jake was faster. He had his hand in it.

"Oh, well, that didn't hurt nothing," he said. "Have to crumble them up to eat 'em anyway." He removed the three cookies that remained whole and handed the sack to Amy. "Here, you and Nicky can divide the rest."

"But you took three," Amy argued. "And you just left the crumbs for Nick and me."

"But I'm company," Jake reminded. "And I'm the biggest. I need the most."

"That's not fair," Nick shouted. "I want a cookie."

"Give him a cookie, Amy," Jake ordered as he shoved one whole cookie into his mouth.

"You give him a cookie!" Amy demanded.

"I'm going to tell Mother." Nick started for the house.

"No, Nick." To everyone's surprise Amy stopped him. "Let Jake have his cookies. Here, we'll share the crumbs."

She opened the sack.

Nick's mouth fell open. Jake hurriedly stuffed the other two cookies into his mouth, almost choking.

Slowly, Amy and Nick ate the crumbled cookies, enjoying every bite. Jake watched. He wanted another bite, but he knew Amy wasn't likely to give him any more without a fight. So he gathered up his toys and went home.

When Nick told his mother about eating the crumbs, she hugged Amy. "You are growing up, Amy," she said approvingly.

"Jake is selfish," Nick stated. "I don't know why Amy wouldn't let me tell on him."

Amy put her chin in her hand. "Well," she said. "I remembered Abram and Lot. Jake was kinda like Lot. He took the best and left the rest for us."

"So?" Nick shrugged.

"So in the end God gave Abram a lot more than Lot took," Amy reminded him.

Nick cast a sly look at the cookie jar. Mother laughed. "All right. I get the point." She slid the cookie jar across the table to the children. "Help yourself."

The Reason:

(Riddle answer: He divided the land with Lot.)

Selfishness never pays. In the end, Lot lost everything. (Oops! Shouldn't have told you; that's another story.) And God promised to give Abram everything he could see! What a promise!

- How do you think Abram felt when his nephew took the best?
- How do you feel when someone else takes the best and leaves you the crumbs?
- Have you ever taken the best? Have you ever taken the least? Which made you feel better?

Put self first,
Feel the worst.

17

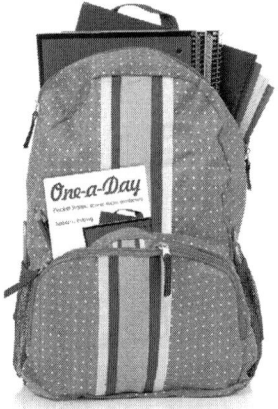

The Lead

He was selfish, but I forgave;
The life of my nephew I did save.
Who am I?

___ ___ ___ ___ ___

Key Verse:
Do not be overcome by evil, but overcome evil with good (Romans 12:21).

Scripture Reading:
Genesis 14:8-16

Joy slammed her books on the kitchen bar. "Jennifer Christy got the lead in the school play."

Mrs. Morgan looked up. Joy's freckles were popping. "Why are you so angry about it, honey?" she asked.

"She cheated!" Joy exploded. "We had tryouts and then Miss Parker let the kids vote. Jennifer passed the word around that everyone who voted for her to be the princess could go swimming in her family's new pool."

"Oh. . . ." Mrs. Morgan raised her eyebrows.

"I did the part a lot better than she did!" Two hot tears rolled down Jennifer's cheeks. "Just because she's pretty and rich . . . it's not fair."

"No, it's not," her mother agreed. "Life hardly ever is. But how we react to these unfair situations determines whether we become a bitter or a better person."

"Oh,.Mother, don't preach at me now," Joy sobbed.

Mrs. Morgan gathered the disappointed little girl in her arms. "I'm sorry, honey. Just try not to be bitter. When all is said and done, you will come out in the lead."

"But, Mother, I told you Jennifer got the lead. There's no way I can get it now," Joy choked.

"I don't mean the lead in the play," Mrs. Morgan explained. "I mean the lead in life. You will come out ahead if you will keep a good attitude about this."

The next couple of weeks Joy did her best to be kind to Jennifer, but it wasn't easy. Jennifer stumbled and stammered through every play practice. Most of the students laughed at her behind her back.

"She's going to ruin the whole play and make us all look stupid!" Natalie raged. "It's too bad you didn't get the part, Joy. You're good at memorizing."

Joy bit her lip. It was hard not to say what she was thinking.

Miss Parker was losing patience. "Jennifer, you've got to learn your part!"

Jennifer burst into tears. "I can't do it, Miss Parker!"

Miss Parker frowned. "You've got to. It's too late to get anyone to replace you." She looked at the class. "Will anyone volunteer to help Jennifer?"

No one raised their hand. Miss Parker repeated the request. Finally, Joy raised her hand. Miss Parker gave a sigh of relief. "Oh, Joy, that's great. Thank you."

For the next week Joy spent every spare moment coaching Jennifer. By the afternoon of the program, Jennifer was ready.

Joy watched from the sidelines as Princess Jennifer took the center of the stage with her court around her. *She's a much prettier princess than I would have been,* Joy thought. Then she realized with amazement that she was not jealous.

When the play was over, Jennifer ran from the stage and grabbed Joy. "Oh, Joy, thank you! I could never have done it without your help. I don't know why you did it when I practically stole the part from you, but I thank you. You're the best friend I ever had."

Then Joy understood what her mother had said. She had lost the lead in the play, but she had gained a friend. Yes, she had come out ahead.

The Reason:
(Riddle answer: Abram)

Returning good for evil is not easy. But it is always best.
- How do you think Lot felt when his Uncle Abram rescued him?
- How does it make you feel when someone you have been hateful to is kind to you?
- Have you ever returned good for evil? How did it make you feel?

Be better, not bitter.

18

Don't Rush It

You can't speed it up;
You can't slow it down;
Till eternity begins
It'll always be around.
What is it?

___ ___ ___ ___

Key Verse:
They soon forgot His works; they did not wait for His counsel (Psalm 106:13).

Scripture Reading:
Genesis 16:1-16

As Russell followed Grandfather Garrison down the garden row, a loud VVVVRROOM drowned out their words. Russell's eyes fastened on the cycle racing down the gravel road.

"One of these days I'm going to have a motorcycle," he dreamed.

"I hope not," Grandfather frowned. "They're too dangerous. That Nelson kid is only thirteen. He doesn't even have a license."

Russell kicked a clod of dirt. "I don't see why he should have to wait to get a license. He knows how to drive it. Grown-ups are always telling us kids to wait." He mimicked his mother's voice. "'Wait until you're older. Wait until Christmas. Wait for your turn.' I get tired of waiting."

Grandfather nodded. "I know, but rushing things can be dangerous and disappointing."

The boy decided to change the subject. "I'm hungry for watermelon. This one looks good." He stooped to pick it.

"Wait!" Grandfather thumped the melon. "That one isn't ripe yet. It will be a few more days before it is ready."

"But it looks good to me," argued Russell. "And I'm hungry for watermelon now. I don't want to wait."

Grandfather shrugged, "OK. Go ahead and pick it."

"Whoooppeee!" Russell broke off the stem. "It's a big one! But I can carry it. Let's go. I'm hungry."

When they brought the melon into the house, Grandmother thumped it. "Why, Bob, this melon isn't. . . ."

Grandfather shook his head and she hushed. "Russell wants it right now. He doesn't want to wait."

Grandmother raised her eyebrows. "Then I guess he doesn't want to wait for it to cool in the refrigerator?"

"I sure don't," Russell declared. "Let's eat."

"OK," Grandfather agreed as he took a large knife from a drawer. "Here goes." He plunged the knife deep into the heart of the melon and pulled it around the melon's center. With a crisp crunch the melon fell open.

Russell frowned. "It's not very red, but it'll be good."

Rrrrinnnnggg. "I'll get it." Grandmother left the room to answer the phone.

Grandfather handed Russell a slice of melon. The boy looked up. "Aren't you going to eat any?"

Grandfather chuckled. "I think it'll be a couple weeks before I'm hungry for watermelon." The chuckle died on his lips as Grandmother entered the room, looking pale and shaken. "Why, Sarah, what's the matter?"

"The Nelson kid lost control of his motorcycle when the Wilson's dog ran out in front of him." Grandmother knelt beside a kitchen chair. "We need to pray for him right now. He's badly hurt."

After they had prayed, Grandfather picked up the melon. "Guess I'll throw this thing out. Some things you just can't rush, like growing watermelons."

Russell nodded. "I know, and growing up. Like Grandpa said, 'Rushing things can be dangerous and disappointing.'"

The Reason:
(Riddle answer: time)

Abram and Sarah could not wait for God to fulfill His promise and give them a son. They decided to rush things. Abram had a son by Hagar. It was the beginning of much trouble. Waiting for God's time is not always easy, but it is best.

- Is there something you want to do now but your parents or those in authority are saying, "Wait"?
- Why are they making you wait?
- What would be the advantages of waiting?

If God says, "Wait,"
Child, don't debate.

19

Entertaining Strangers

What did the leg say to the brain?

Key Verse
Do not forget to entertain strangers, for by so doing some have unwittingly entertained angels (Hebrews 13:2).

Scripture Reading:
Genesis 18:1-16

Bryan threw his pencil down. "I'll never get this math!"
Mrs. Harmon came into the room. "Yes, you will."
Mr. Harmon peered over his paper. "Who called?"
"Pastor Wilson. He said a lady from the southeast corner of the state is bringing her son to the city for six weeks of intense physical therapy. The boy, Wendell, was injured in a car wreck several months ago. He lost a leg and is being fitted with an artificial one. They can't afford to stay in a motel and eat out for six weeks."

Bryan knew what was coming next. They had two empty bedrooms. "How old is this kid?" he asked.

"A year older than you: fourteen," his mother answered. "Well?"

"OK with me," Mr. Harmon shrugged.

"Bryan?" Mrs. Harmon left the question hanging. Bryan groaned. His mother continued, "Do we keep them or not?"

Bryan rolled his eyes. "I suppose so. But I can't say I'm looking forward to entertaining a crippled stranger for six weeks. I've got my own plans, you know."

The next Monday when Bryan came in from school, Mrs. Wright and Wendell were moved in. Bryan shook hands with them but kept his eyes turned away from the wheelchair.

"We don't want to disturb your schedule," Mrs. Wright said. "Don't feel that we have to be entertained."

Bryan picked up his notebook. "I do have a lot of homework," he explained, still not looking at Wendell. "See you at dinner."

Later at the desk in his room, he buried his face in his hands and groaned, "I'll never get it!"

"Get what?" asked a voice at the door.

Bryan jumped and turned. Wendell was parked in the doorway. Quickly Bryan looked away. "This crazy math."

"Do you mind if I come in?" Wendell asked. "I might be able to help you. Math is one of my better subjects."

"Come on in," Bryan invited. "I could use some help."

Wendell wheeled into the room and parked beside the desk. By the time Mrs. Harmon called them to dinner, the assignment was almost completed. And Bryan was beginning to relax. "Do you . . . do you need me to help you with. . . . ?"

Wendell grinned, "Well, I could use a hand getting down the step into the dining room. I'd hate to miss dinner."

Six weeks later Wendell walked to the car as Bryan followed, pushing an empty wheelchair. As their departing guests pulled out of the driveway, Bryan said to his mother, "Sure is going to be lonesome without them."

Mrs. Harmon put an arm around her son's shoulders. "The Bible tells us to entertain strangers; some of them are angels."

Bryan chuckled, "Well, Wendell is no angel, I know that for sure. But he is one sharp guy. Thanks to him I'm passing in math. And he taught me something else, too."

"What?" Mrs. Harmon asked, as they walked toward the house.

"Not to be afraid of people with disabilities. Wendell had a leg shortage; I had a brain shortage. We helped each other. Thanks, Mom, for letting them stay here."

The Reason:

(Riddle answer: "Stick with me and we'll go places.")

When Abraham invited three strangers into his tent, he had no idea he was entertaining two angels and the Lord. When we open our homes and hearts to strangers, good things can happen.

- In this day of crime what are some guidelines we can use for determining what strangers to entertain?
- What is the best way to approach the disabled people who come into our lives?

A stranger in need
Can become a friend indeed.

20

Knock Again

What should we do every day? (Unscramble the letters in this puzzle to find the answer.)

___ ___ ___ ___

Key Verse:
Ask, and it will be given to you; seek, and you will find; knock, and it will be opened to you" (Matthew 7:7).

Scripture Reading:
Genesis 18:16-33

As the Wheeler family joined hands, Mr. Wheeler added, "Let's keep praying for Uncle Jeff."

Staci shook her head. "But, Dad, the more we pray for him, the worse he gets. Now he's in prison."

"All the more reason to pray for him," Mrs. Wheeler said.

Staci was not convinced. She bowed her head and prayed with her family, but she didn't pray for Uncle Jeff. She had made up her mind to spend her prayer time on someone else—someone for whom it would do more good.

One afternoon, a week later, Mrs. Wheeler met Staci at the door. "Grandmother Wheeler called, and she has a loaf of fresh bread for us. Would you go get it?"

"Sure, Mom," Staci answered as she jumped on her bike.

At Grandmother's house she knocked loudly. Once . . . twice . . . three times. No answer. She knocked again . . . louder. Still no answer. "Must not be home," she mumbled as she hopped back on her bike and pedaled home.

As she came into the kitchen, Mother was on the phone. "Here she is now," she said. "I'll send her back." She hung up the receiver.

"Grandmother wasn't home," Staci announced.

Mother grinned. "Yes, she was. She was in the back yard. You didn't give her time to get to the door. Now, please run back over there and get that bread. I want it for dinner."

Staci plopped down on the couch. "Let me catch my breath first."

Mother nodded and went out to get the mail. She came back with a letter in her hand. "It's from Uncle Jeff," she said. Quickly, she opened it. As she read, a broad smile spread over her face. "Listen to what he writes. 'I've had a lot of time to think since I've been in here. One of the inmates has loaned me his Bible. I'm beginning to think maybe there is hope for me. Keep praying.'" She folded the letter. "Sometimes we are tempted to quit praying just before the answer comes."

Staci blushed. She felt guilty as she remembered her decision. She jumped up. "Just like I quit knocking before Grandmother got to the door. Guess I'll go try again.

This time I'll keep knocking on Grandmother's door and God's, too, until I get an answer."

The Reason:
(Riddle answer: PRAY)

Abraham prayed for God to spare Sodom because his nephew Lot lived there. Because of Abraham's prayers, Lot was delivered (but that's tomorrow's story). Our responsibility as Christians is to pray for others. If the answer does not come immediately, we must keep praying. God will answer our prayers.
- Have you been praying for someone for a long time?
- How long? Don't give up. Keep praying.

Pray, then
Pray again.

21

Good News, Bad News

My first letter is in MAY, but not in RAY.
My second letter is in GET, but not in GOT.
My third letter is in ROAD, but not TOAD.
My fourth letter is in CAN, but not in MAN.
My last letter is in PAY, but not in PAD.
I am ____ ____ ____ ____ ____.

Key Verse:
Oh, give thanks to the LORD, for He is good! For His mercy endures forever (Psalm 107:1).

Scripture Reading:
Genesis 19:15-30

Craig tossed and turned on his bed. *Why did I go with Chuck? As many times as Mom and Dad have told me to stay away from those guys. . . .* He moaned as hot tears fell on his pillow.

He hadn't done one thing . . . not written one word on the wall . . . not broken one window . . . not slashed one chair. But he had been there. He knew it was only a matter of time before Pastor Collins caught up with them. Already, the finger of suspicion was pointing at Chuck and his gang. *And everybody knows you were with them,* Craig's conscience reminded. *Everybody but your mom and dad. They think you were visiting with old Mr. Farmer. Good old Craig, visiting the elderly.*

Craig stuffed the pillow over his head. *Hush! Hush!* His mind screamed. *Leave me alone! I didn't do anything.*

Oh, no, continued his conscience, *good old Craig didn't do anything . . . just disobeyed his parents and lied to them and. . . ."*

"Stop!" Craig screamed as he jumped out of bed and ran sobbing into his parents' room.

"What in the world?" asked Mr. Lawrence as he sat up in bed and switched on the light.

Choking and crying, Craig poured out the whole story. He had thought they were only going to play basketball on the church parking lot. He knew his parents didn't approve of Chuck so he had told them he was going over to Mr. Farmer's. When he realized the boys intended to vandalize the church, he was afraid to leave and afraid to stay.

"Oooohhhh, Dad, what am I going to do?" Craig wailed.

Mr. Lawrence put his arm around the shaking shoulders. "We are going to see Brother Collins in the morning and tell the truth," he answered.

Craig looked up at his dad. "W-w-we are?"

Mr. Lawrence nodded. "I'm going with you."

The next morning they sat in Pastor Collins's office as Craig confessed his part in the vandalism. Solemnly, his pastor asked, "Who was with you, Craig?"

Craig gulped. "Do I have to tell you, sir?"

Brother Collins shifted in his chair. "No, you don't. I already know. In fact, I was going to call your father this morning."

Craig's eyes widened. "You do believe me, don't you, Brother Collins? I didn't do a thing."

Pastor Collins frowned. "I believe your story, Craig. But you did do something. You rebelled against your parents. You disobeyed them. And you lied. You know Chuck's reputation, and you don't belong with those guys." He stood up. "The bad news is that you sinned; the good news is that you confessed. There is mercy for those who confess their sins. Let's pray."

The Reason:
(Riddle answer: mercy)

God sent angels to Sodom with bad news: Sodom was to be destroyed. . . and good news: Lot and his family could be saved. Jesus Christ brought to this earth bad news: all are sinners, and good news: all who confess their sins can be saved.
- Lot suffered for running with the wrong crowd. How did he come to be living in Sodom?
- God showed mercy to Lot and his family and offered them deliverance. Why do you think some of Lot's family refused to leave Sodom?
- Jesus is offering salvation to this world today. Why do people refuse His plan?
- Have you repented of your sins? If not, confess them now. Don't wait for them to be revealed at the judgment.

Bad news: Judgment is coming.
Good news: Mercy is here.

22

Just Wait

Put these letters "AIT"
In the blanks to finish this important message.
F___ ___ ___h w___ ___ ___s.

Key Verse
For you have need of endurance, so that after you have done the will of God, ye may receive the promise (Hebrew 10:36).

Scripture Reading:
Genesis 21:1-8

As Grandfather Hale dropped the seeds into the furrow, Kirby followed on his knees, covering them gently.

"Dinner," called Grandmother from the back porch.

Kirby straightened and wiped the sweat from his brow. Grandfather laughed, "Now there's mud on your face."

At the dinner table Kirby reported, "We planted corn and peas and watermelon."

"Great," Grandmother responded. "Could you gentlemen take me to town after dinner to buy a certain young man's birthday present?"

Grandfather nodded, and Kirby whooped with delight. "Remember you promised to get me a remote-control car." Then he sighed, "I wish it was my eighteenth birthday."

Grandfather chuckled. "And why would that be?"

Kirby grinned. "You know. You promised to buy me a car, a real car, when I'm eighteen."

Grandfather winked at Grandmother. "Now did I really? Grandma, you better start saving your pennies . . . only eight years to go."

On the way to town, Grandmother asked, "Kirby, does your father ever go to church with you and your mother?"

Kirby shook his head sadly. "Never."

Grandmother squeezed the boy's hand. "When your father was a teenager, God promised me that He would continue to draw him to salvation as long as I prayed for him."

The boy sighed. "I must not have any faith."

Grandfather shifted gears. "Why do you say that?"

"Because I've prayed and prayed for Daddy and he's still not saved, so I guess I don't have any faith."

Grandmother turned Kirby's face toward her. "Kirby, do you think God would lie?"

Kirby looked shocked. "Oh, no! God could never lie!"

Grandmother shook her head. "Then you have faith. Faith is simply believing that God will keep His word, that He will not lie. God promised me that He would continue to move on your dad's heart, but He didn't tell me when your dad would surrender his life to Him. So I'm just praying and waiting."

Grandfather slowed for the city limits. "Kirby, this morning we planted seeds in the garden. Now what do we do?"

Kirby looked puzzled. "We don't do anything; just wait."

Grandfather grinned. "That's right. We just wait."

Grandmother nodded. "Your grandpa promised you a car for your eighteenth birthday. Do you follow him around begging him for a car? Do you worry every day, afraid he'll forget?"

"Of course not," Kirby replied. "He won't forget." He grinned, "But it sure is hard to wait."

Grandmother smiled, "I know, but waiting patiently is the test of faith. We keep praying to show God that we are still believing and still waiting, but we don't have to beg Him and we should not doubt His promises."

As Grandfather pulled the pickup into a parking spot, Kirby reached for the door handle. "Let's go get my present. I'm glad we don't have to wait for every promise."

The Reason:
(Riddle answer: FAITH WAITS.)

God has never broken a promise. Abraham and Sarah waited twenty-five years for God to fulfill His promise.
- What is faith?
- Have you ever had to wait for a promise to be fulfilled? Are you waiting for God to keep a promise?
- How can faith keep us from worrying?

Just wait.
God's never late.

23

A New Home for Lowell
noitɔɘjɘЯ

Hold this page in front of a mirror to find one of the saddest words in the world.

Key Verse:
When my father and my mother forsake me, then the LORD will take care of me (Psalm 27:10).

Scripture Reading:
Genesis 21:9-21

Through the thin partition Lowell heard Susie's shrill voice. "Bill, that kid's got to go! He's hateful and mean."

"B-b-b-but, S-s-s-susie, he's-s-s-s my k-k-k-kid."

Lowell heard his dad's weak, slurred protest. Lowell snorted. He couldn't remember when his dad hadn't been drinking. Nor could he remember his real mother. She had left twelve years ago when he was a baby. Susie was his dad's latest wife.

With an angry jerk, the boy jammed the soiled pillow over his face. He didn't need to hear anymore. He'd heard it before . . . lots of times.

The next morning a car horn reminded him that it was Sunday. He wiped the egg off his mouth with the back of his hand and grabbed his jacket.

Sunday school was the one sunny spot in Lowell's world. He knew he didn't always behave the best in class, but even when he was a pain, Sister Joyce acted as if she liked him.

This morning Lowell was so wrapped up in his problems that he forgot to poke and pick on the kid next to him. He didn't hear the first of the Bible story. But when Sister Joyce started talking about this kid being rejected and turned out of his home, Lowell leaned forward.

"Listen to how God took care of Ishmael." She looked straight at Lowell. From then on, he heard every word. Later as the students filed out of the room, Sister Joyce put a hand on his arm. "Is something wrong, Lowell?"

Tears filled the boy's eyes. He angrily brushed them away. Like water over a spillway, his words gushed out. When he had finished, Sister Joyce put her arm around his shaking shoulders. "God will take care of you, Lowell, just as He took care of Ishmael."

Lowell shook his head. "No. He won't. You don't know how I act at home, Sister Joyce. That other kid . . . he probably didn't act like I do."

Sister Joyce smiled gently. "Didn't you hear the first part of the story, Lowell? The reason Ishmael had to leave home was because he teased and tormented his little brother, Isaac, and made everyone's life miserable. Ishmael was a jealous, rebellious teenager. But God loved him."

Lowell hung his head. "Susie says I'm mean and rebellious."

Sister Joyce nodded. "You may be, but you can change. Lowell, God loves you and has a home for you. After church, we'll talk to Pastor Nelson."

Four months later Lowell moved into his new home, Tupelo Children's Mansion. It was clean and pretty. There were smiles and laughter and hot meals and crisp sheets.

"Dear Sister Joyce," Lowell wrote. "This is the bestest place I ever lived. Could you come and see me? Tell Pastor Nelson that I like it here and everybody likes me. I guess God still takes care of kids like me and Issmal or whatever that guy's name was. I got to go. Rite back. Lowell."

He started to fold the letter and then picked up his pencil again. His face glowed. "P.S. I got the Holy Ghost last night!"

The Reason:
(Riddle answer: rejection)

Ishmael's life was not easy. When Isaac was born, bad things became worse. Finally, Ishmael and his mother were turned out of their home by Sarah. Abraham was grieved, but God promised, "I will take care of the boy." And He did. Ishmael's descendants became a great nation.

- Do you have a friend who has been rejected by a parent or stepparent? How can you help him or her?
- Are you familiar with Tupelo Children's Mansion? Ask your parents or pastor what you can do for this ministry.
- If you have a happy home, stop right now and thank God. Then write a thank-you note to your parents.

God loves you,
No matter what you do.

24

The Truce

What did the scissors say to the cloth?

Key Verse:
Blessed are the peacemakers, for they shall be called sons of God (Matthew 5:9).

Scripture Reading:
Genesis 21:22-34

"Are Uncle Mike and Aunt Linda coming to the family reunion?" Lori asked.

"Certainly," Mrs. Johnson replied.

"Do I have to go? I could stay with Shelly."

Mrs. Johnson looked shocked. "Why don't you want to go?"

"I can't stand to listen to Stephanie's bragging for two days," Lori grumbled. "Ever since Uncle Mike got a promotion, all she can talk about is their new house, new car, new clothes, blah-blah-blah."

Mrs. Johnson sighed, "Well, you'll have to make the best of it. Grandmother Johnson would be terribly hurt if you didn't come."

So Lori went, determined to stay out of Stephanie's way. Surprisingly, it wasn't too hard. Stephanie always seemed to be somewhere else.

The second day Grandmother Johnson sent word to both girls that she needed their help in the kitchen. They met there for the first time.

"Hi, Steph," Lori said shortly.

"Hi," Stephanie snapped.

As the girls worked in cold silence, Grandmother Johnson frowned. Lori and Stephanie had been best friends since they were toddlers. Now they were acting like strangers. She shook her head. "Girls, this won't do. What's wrong?"

"Wrong?" Lori repeated. "Is something wrong?"

Grandmother sat down at the table. "Sit down, girls." Not looking at each other or at their grandmother, they obeyed. "Why aren't you talking to each other?"

Neither answered. Grandmother looked from one to the other. "We'll start with you, Stephanie. Why are you mad at Lori?"

Stephanie cleared her throat. "Well . . . I . . . uhhhh . . . I'm not really mad at her." She hesitated, and then blurted out, "I'm just sick to death of her bragging."

Lori looked at her cousin in shock. "My bragging?"

Stephanie glared at her. "Yes, your bragging." She mimicked Lori, "'I made the honor roll . . . I'm president of my class . . . I sang the lead in the choir. Blah-blah-blah!'"

Lori burst out giggling. Grandmother and Stephanie stared in surprise. Lori was laughing so hard she had to hold her sides.

"Would you please tell us what is so funny?" Grandmother requested firmly.

Lori caught her breath. "I didn't want to come because I'm sick of Stephanie's bragging about her new house, new car, new clothes, blah-blah-blah." Lori dissolved into giggles again.

Stephanie stared at her cousin; then she started giggling. Grandmother joined them. When they finally caught their breath, Lori said, "I know what let's do, Steph. When either one of us starts to brag, the other one should say, 'Blah-blah-blah.'"

Grandmother nodded. "That sounds like a good truce."

"Truce?" Stephanie asked. "What's that?"

Lori wrinkled her nose. "You don't know what a truce is? It's an agreement. I learned that last year."

"Blah-blah-blah," Stephanie giggled.

In the living room Lori's mother looked at Stephanie's mother. "I don't know what's so funny in the kitchen, but I gather the girls have made their peace."

The Reason:

(Riddle answer: "Let's make piece.")

Abimelech knew Abraham would make a better friend than enemy. Abraham felt the same way about Abimelech. So they settled their differences and made a truce.

- Friends are important. If you have to swallow your pride to keep someone's friendship, do it.
- Do you need to make a truce with someone? Do it today.

Don't fuss. Don't fight.
Make things right tonight.

25

Giving Till It Hurts

- FTNERI = _ _ _ _ _ _

Work this rebus to find the secret of getting.
Artwork of rebus

Key Verse:
I will freely sacrifice to You; I will praise Your name, O LORD, for it is good (Psalm 54:6).

Scripture Reading:
Genesis 22:1-14

On the way home from Sunday school, Jessica leaned over the front seat. "What's a sacrifice?" she asked.

Mrs. Hill turned to face her. "It is something we give that costs us a lot. It is giving that hurts."

As they passed a large house on the hill with a fancy "R" engraved on the gate, Mark said, "Just the thought of giving probably hurts Old Mister Moneybags. He never comes when we have a missionary service."

"Mark!" Mr. Hill looked at his son in the rear-view mirror. "His name is Mr. Richman."

"Same thing," Mark muttered.

Mr. Hill raised his voice a fraction. "Mark!"

"Yes, sir. I'm sorry," Mark said half-heartedly. "Anyway, I doubt if Brother Richman's ever given a sacrificial offering in all his life."

"Have you?" his mother asked.

"But I don't have anything to give or I would," Mark protested.

"Be careful," Mrs. Hill warned. "If you make a vow to the Lord, He expects you to keep it."

That afternoon Mark was playing with his chow puppy, Pepper, when Mr. Richman pulled up to the curb. "Is that a good watchdog?" he asked.

"Yes, sir," Mark replied. "The best."

"Then I'll give you a hundred dollars for him," Mr. Richman offered.

Mark's mouth fell open. He shook his head violently. "Oh, no, I wouldn't sacrifice Pepper for any. . . ." He stopped. The word "sacrifice" startled him. Tears filled his eyes. He knew what he had to do.

That evening at church Mark's heart ached as he put one hundred dollars in an envelope and marked it "Bible school in India." Now he knew what "sacrifice" really meant.

At midweek Bible study, Mr. Richman stopped Mrs. Hill in the church foyer. "Your boy surprised me when he sold me his dog," he said.

Mrs. Hill nodded gravely. "I know. It was the biggest sacrifice of Mark's life."

Mr. Richman looked puzzled. "I don't understand. He didn't have to sell him."

"But he did," Mrs. Hill explained. "He sold Pepper to help build the Bible school in India."

Mr. Richman froze. "He . . . he . . . he did what?" The gray-haired man hesitated. "That's the most powerful sermon I ever had preached to me. If that boy can give up his dog, I can finish that building." He started into the sanctuary and then turned with a smile. "By the way, Pepper's so homesick he won't eat. Tell Mark he'd better come and get his dog before he starves to death."

The Reason:
(Riddle answer: giving)

The hardest test of Abraham's faith came when God asked him to sacrifice his son, Isaac. Abraham passed the test. He was willing to give his most treasured possession to God. Because of Abraham's obedience, he was greatly blessed.

- Have you ever given a sacrificial offering? What was the result of your giving?
- What is the greatest offering we can give God? (See Romans 12:1.)
- What does it mean to give our bodies as "a living sacrifice?"

Givers are blessed;
So give your best.

26

A Plot of Ground

It's called a house, a tent, a robe, a shell.
When we're finished with it, it turns to dust.
What is it?

Key Verse:
Yes, I have a good inheritance (Psalm 16:6).

Scripture Reading:
Genesis 23:1-20

Grandfather Hanson patted his stomach. "Good meal, May." Then turned to his daughter, Anne, and grandchildren, Philip and Penny. "Ma and I bought some property yesterday." He winked at Grandmother. "Yep. Eighty-six years old and this is the first piece of land I ever bought." He turned to his grandson. "We've lived on this farm fer sixty-two years, Philip. Old Mr. Jackson was good to us. He furnished the land, seed, and tools. I did the work. We split the profit. When he died, his son Tom said it looked to him like the plan was workin', no need to change it."

Grandmother picked up the story. "When your Grandpa got too old to work, young Tom said no need

A Plot of Ground

for us to move. Said he'd just rent out the land. We could live in this house long as we wanted to, rent-free. Can't beat that. God's been good to us." She picked up a stack of dishes.

"When the dishes are done, let's ride out and see our land," Grandfather suggested.

An hour later they were bouncing down a gravel road. "Yep, first piece of land May and I ever owned. With seven kids, there never was enough money fer land."

Anne shook her head. "I am amazed at how you did it."

Grandfather chuckled, "Sometimes the bean soup was a bit watery, but we made it. Won't be much left for you though when we're gone, Anne. Just a few old sticks of furniture."

Anne squeezed her dad's arm. "Don't talk like that, Dad. You and Mother have given us a good heritage. You took us to church and gave us a godly example to follow. You've given us a past filled with happy memories. You. . . ."

Grandfather patted her hand. "Now, Anne, don't you go gettin' weepy."

She sniffed. "You didn't need to buy any land for me."

Grandfather chuckled. "I didn't. It ain't very big. I hope you're not disappointed."

Penny looked her grandfather straight in the eye. "Gramps, you've got that twinkle in your eyes. You're up to something."

Grandfather laughed. "Penny, you're just like your grandma. Never could pull one over on her." He turned to his daughter. "Turn in the gate at the top of the hill."

"Grandpa!" Philip exclaimed. "That's the cemetery."

"Yep," the old man agreed. "Bought two lots, one fer your grandma and one fer me."

When they stood on the crest of a little knoll, Penny sniffed loudly. Grandfather turned to her. "Now, young lady, don't you go a-cryin'. I brought you up here to tell you somethin'. When I die and they bring me up here, you remember that ain't your grandpa in that box. That's just the old worn-out shell he lived in fer many years. I'll have my brand-new body and be on the other side with my Lord, singing in the angels' choir by then." He looked at the ground under his feet and grinned. "Only piece of land I ever owned on this earth—two cemetery plots."

Anne put her arms around her father. "You've a mansion on the other side, Dad."

The old gentleman hugged her. "Yep! When it comes right down to what's important, guess I've invested in the right things, my heavenly home and my kids."

The Reason:
(Riddle answer: our body)

God promised Abraham the land where he walked, yet all he owned in Canaan in his lifetime was a cemetery. But Abraham had invested in things that counted. After his death, his descendants reaped the benefits of their father Abraham's faith.

- Do you have grandparents who have been a godly example for you? Make a list of important things they have taught you.
- Write them a note of appreciation today, and stick the list in with it.

Death's just a door
Into life forevermore.

27

Birds of a Feather

Who arranged the first blind date in the Bible?

Key Verse:
Do not be unequally yoked together with unbelievers. For what fellowship has righteousness with lawlessness? (II Corinthians 6:14).

Scripture Reading:
Genesis 24:1-4, 10-20

"But I've told you I'm not going to marry Steve. I just want to have some fun." Evie's angry words filled the house.

"They're at it again," Lanny told his parakeet, Merri.

"All that fussing over a boyfriend." The bird leaned her head to one side and chirped. "I'll be glad when you learn to talk," Lanny said. "If you ever do."

Merri hopped off her perch onto the floor of her cage. She was tired of being nagged at about talking, as if talking was the most important thing in the world. Seemed to her that people talked too much. Like now. . . .

"You know what happened to Aunt Lily because she married out of the church." Mrs. Gibson's words came down the hall.

"I've told you and told you, I'm not going to marry Steve. Even if I did, he's not like Uncle Charles. I just want go to the spring festival with him," Evie argued.

"No, Evie," Mr. Gibson's firm reply drowned out the girl's sobs. "You cannot date an unbeliever."

BANG! A door slammed. Silence followed.

The five-year-old frowned at the bird. "Do you ever get lonely in that cage, Merri? Would you like company?"

Tweet-tweet, the parakeet chirped.

Lanny nodded. "OK. I'll see what I can do about it."

A week later Evie was greeted by a terrible commotion when she came in from school. "What in the world?" she raced down the hall. Lanny was standing beside Merri's cage looking worried. Inside, two birds were going crazy.

"Lanny! What's that bird doing in Merri's cage?"

The little boy stuck his finger in his mouth. "I . . . I . . . Merri wanted some company. So I caught this bird in the birdhouse and brought it in here to visit her and . . . and I guess they don't like each other."

Evie's eyes snapped. "I think not. Sparrows and parakeets don't go together." She opened the cage door. Out flew two very frightened birds. "Now, we've got to figure out how to get that sparrow out of here. Where is Mother?"

"Next door, cutting out a dress for Mrs. Jones," Lanny called as he ran into the next room, following the birds. The sparrow had just flown out the window, and Merri lay trembling in the bottom of her cage when Mrs. Gibson came home. "What happened?" She surveyed the damage.

"Lanny decided Merri needed some company so he brought a sparrow in and put it in her cage!" Evie raged. "Of all the dumb things to do." She shook her finger at the boy. "Don't you know better than to put a wild bird with a tame one?"

Mrs. Gibson closed the window and then turned to her daughter. "And, Evie, don't you know better than to think a Christian can date a sinner?"

Evie collapsed on the couch in tears. "I know, Mother, I know." Mrs. Gibson sat down beside her. "I was going to tell Steve today that I would go to the festival with him. I planned to lie to you and say I was at Kelli's. Then I heard Steve and Paul talking about going into the peep shows at the carnival and getting Paul's big brother to buy some beer, and I knew I couldn't do it."

As mother and daughter talked softly, Lanny went to check on Merri. As he entered the room, the parakeet flapped her wings and twitted, "Naughty, naughty, naughty."

Lanny's eyes sparkled. "Mother! Evie! Come quick! Merri's talking."

The Reason:
(Riddle answer: Abraham's servant)

Isaac was to be the father of a great nation. Abraham knew it would never do for the mother of that nation to be a Canaanite, so he sent his servant to find Isaac a wife from his family in Haran.
- What is the danger of a believer dating an unbeliever?
- Why is it important for Christians to marry Christians?

Winners don't date sinners.

28

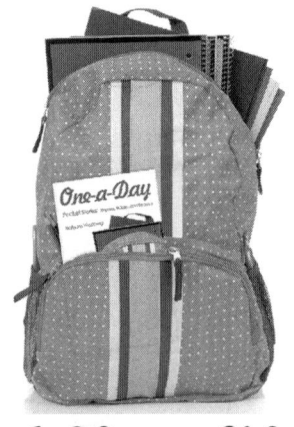

A New Life

I am a walking water barrel.
What animal am I?

____ ____ ____ ____ ____

Key Verse:
I have come that they may have life, and that they may have it more abundantly (John 10:10).

Scripture Reading:
Genesis 24:34-51, 58-67

"We're going to church?" the twins echoed. They couldn't believe their ears. Their family never went to church.

Mrs. Conners nodded. "Go change your clothes."

"Are we going to Aunt Sarah's church?" Nathan asked.

Again their mother nodded.

"Whoopeee!" they yelled as they raced for the bathroom.

Later as they waited on the porch swing for their parents, Naomi asked, "Nat, do you think Mom and Dad might join Aunt Sarah and Uncle Matt's church?"

Nathan shrugged. "Never know about them."

Fear darkened Naomi's eyes. "Are they going to get a divorce?"

Her brother looked away. He didn't answer.

Naomi sniffed loudly. "If we go to that church, will our family be like Aunt Sarah's?"

"What do you mean?" Nathan asked.

Naomi gave the swing a shove with her toes. "Well, you know they're . . . they're different. They don't go to the movies. Lisa always wears dresses. Aunt Sarah doesn't smoke, and Uncle Matt never gets drunk."

Nathan looked back. His eyes were watery. "If we joined their church, I guess we'd be like that too. Why? Don't you want to?"

"Want to?" Naomi took a deep breath. "I want to more than anything in the world."

On the way home from church, Nathan poked his sister and whispered, "Look! They're holding hands."

Their parents were talking so excitedly that they did not hear the conversation in the back seat. "What happened to them up there at the altar?" Naomi asked behind her hand.

"They got the Holy Ghost," Nathan whispered back. "Aunt Sarah explained it all to me. They won't get a divorce now. Don't worry."

Naomi sank back with a sigh of relief. "And our family will be like Aunt Sarah's."

When they arrived home, the twins sat down on the couch between their parents. "Things are going to be different around here," Mr. Conners promised. "No more smoking, no drinking, no cussing, no wild parties. . . ."

Mrs. Conners added, "No feudin', fightin' and fussin'."

Nathan looked across the room. "No TV?"

His father screwed up his face. "I hadn't thought of it, but I guess not. If we aren't going to smoke and drink and fight, we don't need to watch other people do it in our living room."

Naomi looked at her mother. "No shorts, no jeans, no makeup for us girls?"

"No shorts, no jeans, no makeup," Mrs. Conners agreed.

Naomi turned to Nathan. "We are going to be like Aunt Sarah and Uncle Matt's family. Happy!"

The Reason:

(Riddle answer: camel.)

When Rebekah made the decision to marry Isaac, she left behind her old life, family, and home. Everything she gave up, God replaced with something better.

- How do you think Rebekah felt as she left to go to a strange land? Why do you think she did it?
- Name some things we give up when we live for God.
- Name some blessings we receive when we live for Him.

Out with sin and strife;
In comes abundant life.

29

Let's Trade

To find whom Esau cheated, unscramble the letters in the alphabet stew.

Key Verse:
Lest there be any . . . person like Esau, who for one morsel of food sold his birthright (Hebrews 12:16).

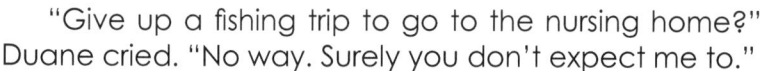

Scripture Reading:
Genesis 25:29-34

"Give up a fishing trip to go to the nursing home?" Duane cried. "No way. Surely you don't expect me to."

Mrs. Johns picked up her purse. "I just told you that Sister Nelson called and asked you to play your guitar at the service Saturday afternoon. It's your decision."

Duane put on his jacket. "Well, I've already made it. I'm going fishing with Joe and his dad Saturday."

Mrs. Johns looked at her watch. "We'd better hurry. We're to be at Uncle Walter's attorney's office at 4:30."

Duane followed his mother to the car. "I wonder what Uncle Walter left me."

Mrs. Johns slid behind the wheel. "Don't count on much. I know most of his estate goes to the Children's Mansion."

"I imagine he left me his electric guitar," Duane dreamed. "He knows . . . knew . . . how much I love music."

At the lawyer's office, Duane took a seat beside his cousin Larry. The attorney cleared his throat and read.

Duane poked Larry and whispered, "Doesn't make much sense to me."

Larry put a finger over his lips. "Sssshhhh."

The attorney was reading, "To my nephew Duane, I leave my coin collection."

Larry looked disappointed. "I wanted that," he hissed.

"And to my nephew Larry, I leave my electric guitar," the attorney continued.

Duane whispered, "And I wanted that."

A warning look from their mothers hushed them. After the reading, the boys made a dash out the door.

"Let's trade," Larry suggested. "My guitar for your coins."

Duane nodded. "Sounds like a good idea." He hesitated, "But I'd better ask my mother first."

On the way home Duane mentioned Larry's offer. Mrs. Johns pushed her glasses up with one finger. "Right now the guitar and the coin collection have about the same value, about $500. Five years from now, the guitar will be worth half as much, maybe $250, and the coin collection could easily be worth $1,000."

"Wow!" Duane exclaimed.

Mrs. Johns continued, "It's a matter of whether you are more interested in enjoying the guitar now or investing in the future."

"Hummmm . . ." Duane mused. "A coin collection is not much fun, but by the time I'm ready for college, it could be pretty valuable. On the other hand. . . ." His words faded.

The phone was ringing as they walked into the house. Duane answered. "Hello . . . Oh, hi, Larry. Yeah, I asked her. She said I could do what I wanted to do about it. I've decided not to trade. I don't want to be like Esau. . . . You don't know about Esau? Well, next time you're over here, remind me and I'll tell you about him. Bye."

As soon as he hung up, the phone rang again. "Hello. . . . Oh, hi, Sister Nelson. . . . No, I don't think I can. I've planned to go fish. . . . Wait. I just changed my mind. I'll trade a fishing trip for a visit to the nursing home after all. See you there. Bye."

On Saturday afternoon Duane ran through the pouring rain into the nursing home. He grinned at Sister Nelson who stood waiting. "Mark me up another right choice."

The Reason:

(Riddle answer: HIMSELF)

Isaac was a very rich man. Esau's birthright as the oldest son entitled him to twice as much of his father's goods as Jacob. He sold all that for one bowl of bean soup.
- Why do you think Esau made such a foolish trade?
- Many kids are interested only in having a good time now. What are some ways you can plan for the future?
- What are some things you might have to give up today to prepare for tomorrow?

Right choices today;
Tomorrow will pay.

30

It Takes Two to Fight

What is the best way to destroy your enemies?

Key Verse:
When a man's ways please the Lord, He makes even his enemies to be at peace with him (Proverbs 16:7).

Scripture Reading:
Genesis 26:12-22

Alicia skidded to a stop between two swings. "Got us some swings, Megan," she yelled. But just as she reached to grab them, she was shoved aside by Mike, the third-grade bully. "Not so fast, little girl. These swings are taken."

"They are not!" Alicia howled as she stumbled.

An ugly grin covered Mike's face. "Are too. I just took 'em."

Megan ran to Alicia's aid. "Give her back those swings!'

"Make me!" countered Mike as he jumped into one swing and held the other tightly in his fist. "Hey, Joe," he called across the school yard. "I got us two swings."

Alicia pulled on the empty swing. "Help me, Megan."

Megan reached for the chain, then she remembered the story of Isaac her dad had read last night in family devotions.

"Stop, Alicia," Megan ordered. "Let's go teeter-totter."

Alicia shrugged and followed Megan. Just as they reached the teeter-totters, a familiar voice said, "Sorry, girls. We want this one."

"Oh, no, you don't!" Alicia screamed. "Go away, Mike Burns. This is our teeter-totter."

"You mean it *was* your teeter-totter," Mike mocked. "It's mine and Joe's now."

Alicia's dark eyes snapped. "Come on, Megan. Let's go tell Miss Anderson." She grabbed Megan's hand and pulled.

But Megan didn't budge. She was thinking. "No, Alicia, let's don't."

Astonished, Alicia argued, "Let's do." She started toward the building in a huff.

"Stop, Alicia!" Megan ran after her. "I want to tell you something." She led her friend to the steps, and they sat down. As Megan told Alicia the story of Isaac and the wells, an idea formed in her mind. "Let's play like we're Isaac and Mike and Joe are the Philistines."

Alicia grinned, "That'll be fun."

Megan stood up. "Now remember, don't fight back when you start to get mad. Just move on."

The girls had started to pump the swings when Joe grabbed them. "Scoot, gals. Me and my buddy are gonna swing."

Megan and Alicia giggled. "OK." They slid out of the swings.

The boys blinked. Then Joe growled, "Guess they're finally getting smart, Mike. They know it won't do any good to fight with us."

Between giggles, Megan gasped, "Come on, Isa . . . I mean, Alicia. Let's go climb the monkey bars."

The boys followed the giggling girls. "I don't see what's so funny," Mike complained. "And you just stay off the monkey bars. We're gonna climb 'em."

"OK, Mr. Philis. . . . ," Alicia clamped a hand over her mouth and doubled up in laughter.

"Phyllis? My name ain't Phyllis! It's Mike."

"Awwww, come on, Mike." Joe grabbed his buddy's arm. "Let's go play ball. It ain't no fun fightin' these dumb girls. All they can do is giggle."

As the boys stomped across the playground, Megan jumped up and down. "It worked! It worked!"

Alicia's dark eyes sparkled. "Well, Isaac, what do you want to do, swing or teeter-totter or climb the monkey bars?"

The Reason:

(Riddle answer: Make them your friends.)

Isaac was a peaceful man. He would not fight for his rights. Because Isaac's ways pleased the Lord, the Lord made his enemies to be at peace with him.

- Have you ever been in a fight, a knock-'em-down fight? How did it make you feel?
- Have you ever walked away from a fight? How did that make you feel?
- Is it right to fight for your rights? Ask your parents what they think about it.

A fight won't make things right.

31

Disguised

I'm a lion by night,
An angel in light.
Who am I?

___ ___ ___ ___ ___

Key Verse:
Lest Satan should take advantage of us; for we are not ignorant of his devices (11 Corinthians 2:11).

Scripture Reading:
Genesis 27:1-29

"But, Mother," Tyson argued, "it's a Bible story, a Christian movie. Just because it's at the theater. . . ."

Mrs. Brown unplugged the sewing machine. "Son, just because it is at the theater is not the only reason I won't let you go to that movie, although that is one reason. I read a review of it the other day. There are thirty-six scenes or quotations in that one movie that are in direct conflict with the Word of God. The actors and actresses live ungodly lives. And furthermore, we do not go to movies."

The set of his mother's mouth told Tyson "that was that."

But his whole class was going. He didn't want to be the odd man out. "Just this once won't. . . ." he began.

A shrill little voice interrupted, "Mommy, is my costume finished?"

Tyson stomped from the room as Mrs. Brown smiled at the little girl. "Just this minute, Lindy."

A few minutes later a two-legged bear ran into Tyson's room. "GGGGGGrrrrrr!" roared a familiar voice.

"GRRR yourself!" Tyson snapped.

The "bear" advanced with curled paws. In a deep voice it stated, "I'm going to eat you up."

"Go away and leave me alone, Lindy," Tyson ordered.

"I'm not Lindy. I'm a big, mean, old bear."

"Ha!" Tyson snorted. "You don't fool me one bit. Now go scare someone else who doesn't know you."

Lindy sniffed, "You could at least play like you're scared."

As the little girl . . . oops, the bear . . . ran from the room, Mrs. Brown entered and sat down beside Tyson on the bed. "Son," she said, "the devil has lots of costumes."

Tyson's mouth fell open. "Huh?"

She nodded. "He's a master of disguise. He has fooled a lot of people. The Bible calls him a lion, a wolf wearing a sheep's clothing, even an angel."

"An angel?" Tyson echoed.

"Yes," his mother continued. "Satan was once an angel, you know, so that disguise comes natural to him. He can make himself look mighty good. One of his favorite costumes is his Christian suit."

Tyson twisted. He knew what was coming next.

"Just because something is labeled Christian doesn't make it Christian." His mother stood up. "You recognized that 'bear' who came in here a while ago because you know Lindy. The Bible tells us to not be ignorant of Satan's devices. I think we could translate that to include disguises."

"GGGGRRRRR!" A little brown bear came roaring into the room.

Tyson jumped up with a yell. "Oooohh! Look, Mother! It's a bear! Run for your life!" He ran from the room with a giggling bear close behind.

Mrs. Brown followed with a smile. Tyson hadn't said so, but she was pretty sure he had gotten the message.

The Reason:
(Riddle answer: Satan)

Jacob was able to fool his father because Isaac was blind. The enemy would like to blind us so we will not recognize him. But the Word of the Lord pulls the mask off Satan.

- Have you ever worn a costume, pretending to be someone else? Did you fool anyone?
- False prophets (preachers who do not preach the truth) are called "wolves in sheep's clothing." What does this mean?
- In which way do you think Satan is more dangerous, as a lion (roaring and threatening) or an angel (gentle and appealing)?

Learn quick
Satan's tricks.

32

The Spoiled Brat

We're one set, yet we're two:
Moms love us; Dads do too.
What are we?

___ ___ ___ ___ ___

Key Verse:
Behold, I set before you today a blessing and a curse (Deuteronomy 11:26).

Scripture Reading:
Genesis 27:30-41

Mrs. Casey knelt beside her wiggling daughter. "Stand still, Jodi," she mumbled, her mouth full of straight pins. "I don't want to stick you."

Jodi stopped twisting. "I wish this dress was dusty blue instead of rose. When are you going to redecorate my bedroom, Mother? You should see Kendra's room. It's lovely. Mrs. Martin bought Kendra new drapes, new spread, new. . . ."

"Stand still, Jodi!" Mrs. Casey repeated.

Jodi frowned at her reflection in the full-length mirror. "Can't you make the collar bigger, Mom? You aren't going to put a ruffle on the sleeves, are you?"

Mrs. Casey took a deep breath. "Jodi, do you want this dress or not?"

Jodi sighed. "I suppose so. Everybody will have a new dress for Easter. But I'd rather have a store-bought one than a homemade one. Kendra got hers at Dillard's."

Mrs. Casey's face darkened. "Go take this dress off!"

Jodi looked puzzled. *Why was her mother so upset?*

She obeyed without a word.

Later she was rereading her favorite Nancy Drew book when her little brother came charging into her room. "Sissy, help me color this poster." He plopped down on the floor and dumped Crayola's around him.

Jodi lay down her book and dropped down beside him. "OK, pal."

A few minutes later Stanley squealed, "Why did you color his hair brown? I wanted it red like mine."

Jodi shrugged. "Too late now. You should have told me."

For some time they colored in silence.

"Now look what you've done!" Stanley glared at her. "You colored his shoes the wrong color." He grabbed the poster and stood up. "I don't like this old poster anyway. I'm going to throw it away." He stomped from the room.

Jodi gathered up the Crayolas, muttering, "That kid is a spoiled brat. I give up my reading time to help him and all he does is gripe. He's never satisfied. He always. . . ." Her words died. She looked at her clean, attractive room. Through the open closet door she saw a rack filled with stylish, pretty clothes.

She found her mother in the living room, dialing the telephone. Jodi sat down at her feet. Mrs. Casey hung up the phone and looked at her with a question mark.

"Momsie," Jodi said. "I'm sorry I've been so . . . so unthankful and grouchy lately. I've been acting like a spoiled brat."

Mrs. Casey kissed Jodi's cheek. "You're forgiven, and just in time, too. I was calling Aunt Julie to see if Mary Lynn wanted your new dress since you don't seem to like it."

Jodi's stood up and gave her mother a bear hug. "I like it, Mom. Really I do." Her eyes widened. "You weren't going to give her my bedroom, too, were you?"

Mrs. Casey laughed. "No, not this time."

The Reason:
(Riddle answer: twins)

Esau sold the birthright to Jacob because he did not appreciate it. It meant no more to him than a bowl of stew. The birthright and the blessing went together like bread and butter. Jacob had the birthright so he wanted the blessing. The way he got it was not right and he paid for that later (another story). Esau lost them both because he did not appreciate what he had until he lost it.

- Count your blessings. Make a list of ten things for which you are thankful.
- Determine to start saying, "I'm glad I've got," instead of "I wish I had."

Don't wait too late to appreciate.

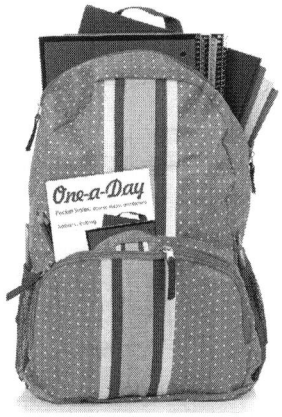

Afraid

Where was Jacob when the lights went out?

Key Verse:
For You, Lord, are good, and ready to forgive (Psalm 86:5).

Scripture Reading:
Genesis 28:10-22

With his head down, Taylor shuffled home from school. He felt like his heart weighed a hundred pounds. His shoulders slumped.

Why did you do it? You know better, a loud voice in his head accused over and over.

As he opened the front door, he straightened his back and pasted on a smile. "Mom," he called, "I'm home."

There was no answer. He glanced at the refrigerator. Sure enough, there was a note. "Be right back. Mother."

"Tippy! Tippy!" Taylor called. No answer. "Tippy! Here, boy." Taylor started down the hall.

Then he saw it. A trail of tissue paper led out the bathroom door and down the hall. "You did it again!"

Taylor scolded the unseen pup. "Where are you? Tippy, come out."

A brown ball of fur came slinking out from under Taylor's bed, tail tucked between his legs. Taylor laughed, "You know you're in trouble. You'd better be glad Mother's not home." He picked up the puppy and held him under his chin. "I love you, Tippy. You're my best friend. Now let's get that mess cleaned up before Mother gets home."

Late that night Taylor tossed and turned on his bed. He couldn't get comfortable. That voice in his head kept repeating, *Why did you do it? You know better.* Taylor pulled the blanket over his head. If he could just hide . . . It seemed like the Lord was standing right beside his bed, looking through the blanket, right inside him. He shivered. It seemed like. . . .

"Mamma! Mamma!" He sat straight up in bed. "Mamma!"

The light came on. Taylor blinked. Mrs. Nelson put her arm around him. "What's the matter Son?"

Wide-eyed Taylor looked around him. "I thought . . . it seemed like . . . I mean. . . ."

"Yes?" his mother questioned.

Taylor shivered. "It seemed like Jesus was here."

Mrs. Nelson nodded. "He is. You know He's always beside you. Why does that frighten you? He loves you."

Taylor gulped. "I . . . I . . . I guess I just . . . I mean I . . . oh, Mamma, I s-s-stole s-s-some money today."

Mrs. Nelson put his face between her hands. "Tell me."

"It was . . . just there . . . on Jason's desk . . . two quarters, and I wanted a Coke so badly . . . and I just took it!" Taylor hid his face in his mother's shoulder.

Mrs. Nelson patted his back. "That's why you were afraid," she said. "The presence of the Lord is frightening when we have sin in our lives. It makes us want to hide."

Taylor thought about Tippy hiding from him.

Mrs. Nelson continued, "It is comforting when we are living right."

Taylor nodded. He knew. Gently, his mother wiped his tears with a tissue. "Tomorrow you can take fifty cents out of your bank and repay Jason." She pulled back the covers. "Now let's pray. The Lord Jesus wants to forgive you."

After they had prayed, Taylor snuggled under the covers and smiled up at his mother. "Thanks, Mom. I'm not afraid anyore."

The Reason:

(Riddle answer: in the dark)

Jacob had lied, cheated, and stolen; now he was running for his life. When he realized he was in the presence of the Lord, he was frightened. But God still loved Jacob. He blessed him and gave him the same promise He had given his grandfather, Abraham. What a good God!

- Does it make you afraid or comforted to know that the Lord is with you?
- Have you ever been afraid when you were in the presence of the Lord (such as in a church service)? Was there sin in your life?
- Whatever you do, God still loves you and wants to bless you. All you have to do to get rid of the fear is confess your sins and ask forgiveness.

Do not fear;
God is near.

34

Not Coincidence

What did the well say to Laban's sheep?

Key Verse:
A man's heart plans his way, but the LORD directs his steps (Proverbs 16:9).

Scripture Reading:
Genesis 29:1-14

Natalie's steps dragged. *First day in a new school is bad enough,* she thought for the umpteenth time, *but first day in middle school in a new town is terrifying.*

Through the trees she could see the roof of the school. Only ten minutes and two more blocks to go. She braced her shoulders and took a deep breath. "Lord Jesus," she whispered, "are You with me?"

A soft breeze touched her cheeks, and she knew He was.

Natalie realized it was right for her family to be in Fort Myers to start a church. But she was so lonely. "All I ask for, Jesus, is one friend. I mean, one friend in addition to You," she prayed as she walked toward the school. Then she chuckled, "I mean, that's all I ask for today. Tomorrow I'll probably need something else."

Natalie had a good relationship with the Lord Jesus. She talked to Him as if He were her best Friend walking by her side . . . which He was.

Just as she reached the corner across from the school, she tripped and fell. "Ooohhh," she squealed. Abruptly, she jumped up. Her palms and knees stung. But one look told her she was not hurt. "My books!" she cried. Her school supplies had scattered in every direction.

"I'll help you," said a strange voice.

Natalie didn't take time to look up. "Thanks," she said as she ran after rolling pencils.

"Here. This is all, isn't it?" asked the stranger as she gave Natalie a handful of supplies.

"I think s-s-so," Natalie caught her breath. Then as she looked at the other girl, she choked. "You . . . you look. . . ."

The other girl giggled. ". . . like you," she finished.

Natalie nodded. "Are you Pentecostal?"

The girl grinned widely. "Sure am. We moved here this summer. My name's Stephanie Winters. What's yours?"

"Natalie McDonald. We moved here this summer, too."

The girls stared at each other. Stephanie said. "Just this morning I prayed that God would give me a new friend. I'm scared to death of starting to a new school alone."

Natalie's eyes widened. "You not only look like me, you are like me."

The peal of the school bell vibrated through the air.

The girls ran toward the building. "It wasn't coincidence that I tripped and dropped my books just as you came up," Natalie said as they climbed the steps. "My

Bible verse for today says that the Lord directs our steps. I guess that means even when we stumble and fall."

Stephanie laughed and opened her notebook. "Let's check our schedules. Wouldn't it be a coincidence if we have the same classes?"

Natalie smiled at her new friend. "Not coincidence. It would be God directing our steps."

The Reason:
(Riddle answer: Nothing. Wells can't talk.)

Jacob decided to go to Haran. God directed his steps, leading him right to the door of an uncle he had never met. God had a plan for Jacob's life, and He has a plan for your life. Things don't just happen to God's children.
- How does it feel to be all alone in a strange place?
- How do you think Jacob felt when he met his uncle and his family?
- Have things ever fallen into place in your life in such a way that you knew God was leading you?

Isn't it neat
How God guides our feet?

35

The Cheater Cheated

Find the three vegetables in this sentence.
"OK" Rachel said to Jacob.
"I hope a swell guy like you will
Be a nice husband."

Key Verse:
Do not be deceived, God is not mocked; for whatever a man sows, that he will also reap (Galatians 6:7).

Scripture Reading:
Genesis 29:15-30

Chip raised his hand. "Miss Berry, may I sharpen my pencil?"

Without looking up, Miss Berry nodded.

On the way back to his seat, Chip detoured past Edwin's desk. Sneaking a look at Edwin's paper, Chip filed the answers to problems 7, 8, 9, and 10 in his brain. Edwin winked at him as he passed.

Back at his desk, Chip quickly filled in the blanks on his test. No need to double-check those answers. Edwin was the class brain. Those four answers with the ones he had worked should give him at least a passing grade.

Miss Berry stood up. "Pass your papers to the front." After she had collected the tests, Miss Berry turned to the class. "Today is the last day for your essays on 'Why I'm Proud to Be an American.' The judging by the American Legion will be tonight, and I'll have a list of winners tomorrow. First prize is twenty-five dollars and second is ten dollars."

Chip took his essay from his notebook. He knew it was good. Most of the material had come from an essay his big brother John had written ten years before at another school.

The next day when Miss Berry handed back the test, Chip couldn't believe his eyes. Answers 7, 8, 9, and 10 were marked wrong. He had failed. When the final bell rang, Miss Berry said, "Chip, please wait."

Chip's heart fell into his socks.

"Chip, on the math test I gave half of the class one set of problems and the other half another set. You got the first set, yet your answers to problems 7, 8, 9, and 10 were the right answers for the second set. Do you have an explanation?"

Chip's tongue thickened. "I . . . I . . . no, ma'am. I . . . I. . . ."

"There's another little problem," Miss Berry continued. "Two of the essays in the contest were very similar, yours and Edwin's."

"Edwin's?" Chip squeaked. "He read John's . . . I mean, he read my essay. He must have copied my ideas."

Mrs. Berry looked doubtful. "Edwin said you copied his. I have never had any problem with him cheating. On the other hand, this is the third time this year that there has been some question about your honesty."

"But, Miss Berry, I'm telling the truth," Chip argued.

Miss Berry frowned. "Your essay was not your writing."

"But, Miss Berry, I didn't steal Edwin's ideas."

The teacher stood up. "Perhaps not, but they didn't come out of your head. I'd like to believe you, Chip, but I can't. The judges have awarded first place prize to Edwin. You may go."

As Chip walked down the hall, he saw Edwin leaning against the water fountain. He clinched his fist. "You stole my essay ideas."

Edwin shrugged. "Your ideas? I was under the impression they were your brother's. Doesn't the cheater like being cheated?" he mocked.

As Edwin swaggered down the hall, Chip muttered, "Your day will come, big boy. Sooner or later, all cheaters get cheated. I know."

The Reason:

(Riddle answers: okra, peas, and bean)

In Haran, Jacob began to reap the seeds he had sown. His Uncle Laban cheated him again and again. Whatever you sow, you will reap. Sow corn; reap corn. Sow kindness; reap kindness. Sow dishonesty; reap dishonesty.

- How do you think Jacob felt when Laban tricked him into marrying Leah? Do you think he realized that he was reaping for tricking his father and brother? Why or why not?
- Do you wonder why people treat you as they do? Have you ever considered how you treat others?
- Do you know someone who is reaping today for something they did in the past?

Cheat today; tomorrow you'll pay.

36

Blessed Because

Jacob's uncle and father-in-law,
Cheating seemed to be my main flaw.
Who am I?

___ ___ ___ ___ ___

Key Verse:
"Blessed is he who blesses you"(Numbers 24:9).

Scripture Reading:
Genesis 30:25-36

Jay had placed the evening paper on the porch when Mr. Akers came out the door.

"Good evening, sir," Jay said respectfully.

Mr. Akers smiled and nodded. "Same to you, son."

Jay pushed up the kickstand on his bike.

"Wait! Wait a minute," Mr. Akers said. "How old are you?"

"Almost fifteen," Jay replied.

"How long have you been our paperboy?" the man asked.

"Two years."

Mr. Akers pursed his lips and nodded. "Hummmmm. You're Jay Jackson, aren't you? Isn't your dad the pastor of the Pentecostal church on Lakeside Drive?"

"Yes, sir." Jay wondered what was next.

Mr. Akers picked up his paper. "You are the best paperboy we have ever had. Would you like to have a job?"

Jay gulped. Mr. Akers didn't know that Jay had been praying for a different job. "Yes, sir, I would."

"I've been needing a boy to help clean up the shop in the afternoons," Mr. Akers said. "Think you'd be interested?"

Interested? Jay was more than interested. Mr. Akers owned Akers' Cycle Sales and Service.

Jay grinned, "Yes, sir!"

Mr. Akers smiled. "You don't happen to have a little brother who could take over this route, do you?"

Jay chuckled. "Yes, sir, I do."

Mr. Akers snapped his fingers. "Then see that he gets it. I want someone I can depend on to deliver my paper. Come in tomorrow afternoon, Jay, and we'll work out your hours."

When Jay was a block away, he let out a big "Hallelujah!" He had a new job and he hadn't even applied for it. He had just prayed about it.

He had been cleaning floors, running errands, and shining cycles for a year when Mr. Akers called him into the office. "Jay," the older man said, "in the past year my business has grown amazingly. You've been good for us."

Jay pointed at himself. "Me?"

Mr. Akers grinned, "Yes, you. You've got lots of friends, you know. And you're always smiling and whistling. The customers like you. The employees like you. I like you. It's time you started learning the ropes of this business. I'm promoting you to part-time junior clerk. And I'm going to give you a raise."

Jay raised his eyebrows. "A promotion? Another raise?"

Mr. Akers nodded. "Another raise." He stood up. "And, son, when you are ready to go to college, let's talk about it. This company just might have a scholarship tucked away somewhere."

Jay couldn't believe his ears. He sat stunned.

Mr. Akers laughed. "I may not be a Christian, Jay, but I'm a smart businessman. I've got sense enough to know that this company has been blessed because you are part of it. I'd like to keep you around."

The Reason:

(Riddle answer: Laban)

God blessed Laban because of Jacob. It pays to associate with God's people. The blessings of the child of God often splash over on others.
- In what ways is your friendship a blessing to others?
- Laban begged Jacob not to leave. Are others glad to have you with them? Why or why not?
- Have you ever been blessed because you were someone's friend? Explain.

Blessings splash like falling rain.
Your friendship can be others' gain.

37

A Change of Plans

Solve this problem to find how many times Laban changed Jacob's wages.

On what day of creation did God rest? ____
Subtract number of sons Noah had. − ____
Multiply by the number of sons Isaac had. × ____
Add daughters of Laban (Jacob's wives).
+ ____
Equals times Laban changed Jacob's wages = ____

Key Verse:
But the LORD has been my defense, and my God the rock of my refuge (Psalm 94:22).

Scripture Reading:
Genesis 31:1-7, 17-18, 22-24, 45-49

With his head down, Paul walked along whistling and kicking a pebble ahead of him. He fingered the coins in his bulging pockets. Finally, he had saved enough to buy the game he wanted so badly.

He turned down the alley that led to the mall's back parking lot. Too late he looked up. Claude and Leo, the sixth-grade bullies, were leaning against a trash dumpster. Paul froze.

"Well, well, look who's coming," Claude guffawed. "Mr. Paul Lawson, the big third-grader. Going to the mall, no doubt, to spend his pennies."

Leo poked his buddy in the ribs. "Yeah, look at those bulging pockets. He's loaded."

Paul rolled his eyeballs. *Should he run? But which way?*

Claude took a menacing step toward the younger boy. "Wonder if he's got enough pennies to buy a can of snuff. I'm flat busted."

Leo took a couple giant steps. "We'll never know till we look. You hold him. I'll search him."

"Jesus, help me," Paul cried as tears rolled down his face.

"Pray all you want, little boy. Just empty your pockets while you do it," Claude mocked, as he grabbed for Paul's arm. "It's time to take the offering."

A voice behind them halted the action. "Got a problem, Paul?" A tall, muscular man stood watching them. They had been so intent they had not seen him walk up.

A smile caught Paul's tears. "Oh, Pastor Stanley, I'm so glad to see you."

Pastor Stanley looked at Claude and Leo who were backing away. "Boys," he said sternly, "if you are thinking about roughing up my friend Paul, I suggest you change your plans."

Without a word, the boys turned and ran down the alley and out of sight.

"On your way to the mall?" Pastor Stanley asked.

Paul nodded. "Yes, sir."

"Then let's walk together," the pastor suggested. He grinned, "I don't usually walk down alleys. But today for some strange reason I could not find a parking place and had to park a block away. So I just happened to take a shortcut through the alley. Strange, huh?"

Paul grinned up at his big friend. "No, not strange. Great!"

Pastor Stanley squeezed Paul's arm gently. "Yep, great! Just like our God! He takes good care of His kids, Paul. Aren't you glad you're one of them?"

The Reason:

(Riddle answer: (7-3) x 2 + 2 = 10. See Genesis 31:7.)

Laban went after Jacob to "get him." But God said, "Change your plans, Laban. Watch what you say to My child." When God's children are in trouble, God comes to their rescue, usually by sending another one of His children to help them.

- Why was Laban angry with Jacob? What do you think he would have done if God hadn't stopped him?
- Can you recall a time when someone plotted against you or your family and God changed their plans?
- God is our defense (protection, guard). How?

One word from God is quite enough
To take the starch out of the tough.

38

Making Peace

What are the hardest two words in the world to say?

Key Verse:
If it is possible, as much as depends on you, live peaceably with all men (Romans 12:18).

Scripture Reading:
Genesis 32:1-20

"This house is a war zone," Mrs. Cline fretted. "Baking, shopping, decorating . . . fussing, quarreling, complaining. Oh, for some peace and quiet."

Amy slammed the door behind her as she stomped into the room. "Now what?" Mrs. Cline asked.

"Guess who got the part of Mary in the Christmas play?" Amy asked sarcastically. "Holly, of course. And she said she didn't even want it! I'm the Reader . . . again!"

Mr. Cline looked up. "Isn't Holly your best friend?"
Amy curled her lip. "She *was* my best friend."
Four-year-old Mindi announced, "I'm an angel."

Big brother Dustin snickered. "If you're an angel, I'm Superman."

"What part did you get, Dustin?" Mr. Cline asked.

"I got a promotion!" Dustin bragged. "I have been promoted from a shepherd to a wise man. No burlap robe for me, folks. I get a bathrobe and a crown this year!"

Everyone laughed but Amy. "Well, I don't even get a costume. The Reader has to stand *behind* the curtain."

She stomped from the room.

Mrs. Cline sighed, "I wonder how the Lord feels about the way we celebrate His birthday?"

A week later as Amy and little sister Mindi helped Mrs. Cline decorate cookies, Mindi practiced her part for the play. "'Glory to God in the high . . . highest, and on earth peace . . . good . . . good will toward men.' Did Mary get Jesus' baby clothes at Goodwill?"

Mrs. Cline laughed. "No, they didn't have Goodwill Industries in Jesus' time."

"When are Aunt Edna and Uncle Carl coming?" Amy asked.

Mrs. Cline frowned. "They aren't. Since Grandmother's gone, there is no reason for us to get together."

"Not coming?" Amy cried. "But it won't be like Christmas. Haven't you spoken to Aunt Edna since Grandmother's funeral? Are you still mad about that album?"

"I'd rather not discuss it," Mrs. Cline answered icily.

"You're mad at Aunt Edna. Amy's mad at Holly," Mindi counted. "I don't know who I'm mad at."

Mrs. Cline sighed as she repeated softly, "'On earth peace, good will toward men.' I could use some peace." She went to the telephone. "I'm going to call Aunt Edna and apologize. It's still not too late for them to come for Christmas."

Amy smiled, "Then I'll call Holly. Maybe she can come over and help us decorate these cookies."

The Reason:
(Riddle answer: "I'm sorry.")

After twenty years of running, Jacob wanted to make peace with his brother Esau. To say "I'm sorry" he sent Esau a peace offering. Saying "I'm sorry" is very hard to do. But it is worth the effort to be on good terms with others.
- How does it make you feel to quarrel with someone you love?
- Why do you think it is so hard to say "I'm sorry"?
- Is there someone you need to apologize to? Do it today.

"I'm sorry" is harder to say
When you delay it day after day.

39

A New Name

What is yours but used most by others?

Key Verse:
Therefore, if anyone is in Christ, he is a new creation (II Corinthians 5:17).

Scripture Reading:
Genesis 32:22-32

"Wait up, Hothead." Hal heard Butch call. "I'll walk with you."

Hal turned and grinned. "I'm waitin'. Hurry up."

Butch ran to catch him. He wrinkled his forehead. "What ya' grinnin' at, Hothead?"

Hal chuckled, "You."

"Me? I ain't funny," the other boy growled. "It's you what's funny, blowin' up at every little thing." Butch laughed. "You shore looked funny yesterday with your face red as fire and your freckles poppin'. What'd Andy say that made you so mad, Hothead?"

Hal shrugged. "I don't remember."

Butch hooked his thumbs in his jean pockets. "Probably nothin'. That's what I mean. You blow up at nothin'."

Hal ignored the other boy's digs. "Are you ready for that history test?"

Butch rolled his eyes. "No way, man. I'm never ready for a test." He eyed Hal. "Say, Hothead, what's with you today, anyway?"

Hal grinned. "Why do you ask that?"

Butch looked puzzled. "I rib you and call you 'Hothead,' and you don't even raise your voice. You just grin and ignore it. Yesterday you'd 'a blowed up."

Hal nodded. "This is a new day and I'm a new guy."

Butch raised his eyebrows. "Oh, yeah? Look like the same guy to me, except. . . ."

"Except what?" Hal prompted.

Butch shook his head. "Nothin'."

Hal shifted his school books to his other arm. "Something great happened to me last night, Butch."

"Yeah? You get a four-wheeler?" Butch questioned.

"No. Something better than that," Hal replied. "I got the Holy Ghost."

Butch stopped and stared at Hal. "The Holy . . . what?"

Hal laughed. "The Holy Ghost. It is the Spirit of Christ that comes into . . . into . . . uhhhh . . . into a person and makes 'em different, like a new person."

"Sounds spooky to me," Butch said.

"But it's not," Hal replied. "It's great. It's exciting!" He looked Butch straight in the eye. "I don't even feel like I did yesterday. I feel . . . I feel happy. I like everybody, even guys that call me 'Hothead.'"

Butch blinked. He quickened his pace. "Come on or we're gonna be late for school."

They walked in silence for half a block while Butch digested Hal's news. Then he said thoughtfully, "You look the same . . . well, almost. You're smilin' and your face is kinda lit up, but mostly you look the same. But you sure ain't actin' the same."

A New Name

Hal jumped over a crack in the sidewalk. "I told you, Butch, I'm a new guy. The Holy Ghost changed me."

Butch stepped on the crack. He looked at his watch. "We'd better run or we're gonna be late, Hot . . . I mean, Hal."

As they broke into a run, Hal chuckled, "See, I even got a new name."

"You do?" Butch puffed.

"Yeah. It's Hal." Hal shifted into another gear. "Race you to the corner."

The Reason:
(Riddle answer: your name)

Jacob's prayer meeting by the brook changed him. Not only did he get a new name, he got a new attitude. Jacob, "the deceiver," became Israel, "a prince with God." When you receive the Holy Ghost, your name will still be Lori or Nathan or whatever your name is. But you will no longer be a sinner but a saint.

- What do others call you behind your back? Or when they are teasing you? What does that tell you about your attitude?
- Have you received the Holy Ghost? If not, you need to do what Jacob did: have a prayer meeting.

All things are new,
When Christ lives in you.

40

The Rusty Box

(To find the answer to this riddle, work this rebus.)

- OGCWA =

You can't measure the pleasure
brought by this treasure.
What is it?
A ___ ___ ___ ___ ___ ___

Key Verse:
Bearing with one another, and forgiving one another, if anyone has a complaint against another; even as Christ forgave you, so you also must do (Colossians 3:13).

Scripture Reading:
Genesis 33:1-16

Kaylene slammed the receiver down. "I'm never going to speak to Heather again!" she raged.

Mrs. Hardin came into the room, putting on her jacket. "Never? Never is a long time, Kaylene."

Kaylene clinched her fist. "But Heather makes me so mad!"

Mrs. Hardin picked up her purse. "Get your jacket. We're going to Grandmother's to help her clean out the attic."

Hours later Kaylene picked up a dusty, rusty metal box. "What's this, Grandmother?"

Grandmother peered over the top of her glasses. "Why, that's my treasure box."

Kaylene shook it. "Treasure box? What's in it?"

Grandmother chuckled. "I can't remember. It was my treasure box when I was about your age. Open it and see."

Kaylene pushed a little lever. "I can't. It's locked."

Grandmother frowned. "No telling where the key is. Run downstairs, honey, and get a screwdriver and hammer."

When Kaylene returned a few minutes later, she handed her grandmother a letter. "The postman just came."

Grandmother sat down on a trunk and opened it. As she read, tears flowed down her cheeks. She choked back a sob. "It's Cecilia. She . . . she . . . Oh, Linda, it's too late!"

Mrs. Hardin put her arm around her mother. "What's too late, Mother? What's wrong?"

Grandmother put her face in her hands. "My only sister, Cecilia, is dead. It's too late to say I'm sorry." Grandmother pulled a tissue from her pocket. "Twenty years ago we quarreled. I . . . I . . . I don't even remember what about. I said I would never speak to her again, and

I . . . I . . . I didn't." Grandmother's shoulders shook. "And now I never will. It's too late . . . too late."

Murmuring words of comfort, Mrs. Hardin led her mother down the stairs. Kaylene followed, carrying the locked box.

Much later, Grandmother said, "Kaylene, you may have the treasure box. Perhaps your dad can open it."

That evening as Mr. Hardin attempted to open the box, Mrs. Hardin remarked, "Every year that Mother and Aunt Cecilia refused to apologize, it became harder and harder to break the silence."

"Like the treasure box?" Kaylene asked.

Mother nodded. "Yes. Stubborn pride locked the lid on their relationship and threw away the key. It's so sad. . . ."

Squeeeeekkkk! "It's opening!" Kaylene squealed.

"What's in it, Dad?"

Mr. Hardin handed her the box. "You look. It's yours."

Kaylene lifted the lid. "Look!" she cried out. "Here's the key. It was locked in the box." She slipped the key into the lock.

"Just like the key to opening the relationship between Mother and Aunt Cecilia was locked within them. They were the only ones who could open it, but they were too proud." Mrs. Hardin stood up. "I'll call Mother and tell her the treasure box is opened."

Kaylene jumped to her feet. "Then I'm going to call Heather. Maybe she'd like to come over."

The Reason:
(Riddle answer: friend)

For twenty years Jacob and Esau were at odds with each other. It was twenty years of lost time when they could have been friends.

- What do you think would have happened if Jacob had apologized to Esau when he first cheated him?
- Are you at odds with anyone? Every day you wait to renew that friendship, it becomes harder and harder. Call or text your friend now. Don't lose any more valuable time.

Make things right before tonight.

41

No Expiration Date

How are God's promises like a steel rod?

Key Verse:
Lo, I am with you always, even to the end of the age (Matthew 28:20).

Scripture Reading:
Genesis 35:1-15

Mrs. Jacobs and her sister, Marcy, sat at the kitchen table sorting coupons. "Marcy, when are you going to get back in church and live for God like you did when. . . .?"

Marcy frowned. "Don't start on that, Marsha. . . ."

She stopped as ten-year-old Kyle came into the kitchen followed by his little sister.

"But, Kyle, you promised. . . ." Ruthie reminded.

"But I don't want to take you to the store," Kyle snapped. "What are you doing?" he asked the women.

Aunt Marcy smiled. "Sorting your mother's coupons. She hasn't cleaned out that cabinet drawer in a year."

Mrs. Jacobs dropped a coupon onto the pile on the floor. Ruthie squatted beside her. "Can I have these, Mamma? I want to play grocery store."

"Sure," Mrs. Jacobs said as she handed her another one.

Kyle stared at the coupon in Ruthie's hand. "Are you going to let her have that, Mother? It's worth one dollar."

Mrs. Jacobs nodded. "It expired last month."

"Half of these coupons have expired," Aunt Marcy added.

"What's 'pired?" Ruthie asked.

"Expired," Kyle corrected. "It means they aren't good anymore." He bit into a cookie. "They're out-dated."

Aunt Marcy held up a coupon. "This is the kind I like. It says, 'No expiration date.' They're good from now until." She winked at Kyle, "And as long as your mother keeps some of these coupons, that could be awhile."

Mrs. Jacobs made a funny face at her sister. Then she turned to Kyle. "Have you fed Mr. Bowman's dog today?"

Kyle grimaced. "Not yet. I didn't know when I promised to feed his dog that he was going to be sick for months."

"That's one of those 'no expiration date' promises," Aunt Marcy said. "Looks like you get to honor your word as long as Mr. Bowman holds you to it."

Ruthie pointed her finger at Kyle. "Kyle promised to take me to the store," she told her mother. "Now he won't do it. He gave me a no-good promise, like these old coupons." Her lower lips trembled.

Mrs. Jacobs frowned at her son. "Kyle, a promise is a promise. Right, Marcy?"

"Right!" Aunt Marcy agreed. "No matter how long ago you made it or how long it takes to keep . . ." She gasped as a funny look crossed her face.

"Do you hurt, Aunt Marcy?" Ruthie asked.

Aunt Marcy's lips formed a crooked smile. "No," she replied. "I just remembered a promise I made a long time ago. It was one of those 'no expiration date' promises."

"What was it?" Kyle asked.

She took a deep breath. "I promised the Lord that I would live for Him."

Kyle's eyes widened. "And you haven't done it!"

Tears filled his aunt's eyes. "No, I haven't. But it's not too late." She turned to her sister. "May I go to church with you tonight, Marsha?"

As the two women hugged and cried, Kyle started out the door. "I'd better go feed Mr. Bowman's dog. When I get back, Ruthie, I'll take you to the store."

The Reason:

(Riddle answer: They cannot be broken.)

When Jacob had his vision at Bethel, he promised to return someday. Over twenty years later, he kept that promise.

- God made Abraham a promise. What was it? (See Genesis 17:3-8.)
- God renewed this promise to Abraham's grandson, Jacob. Where? (See Genesis 28:13-15, 19.)
- God has given us many promises marked, "No expiration date." Can you quote some of them? (How about the Key Verse?)
- What promises have you made to God? Are your promises like steel or glass?

Make no mistake,
God's promises don't break.

42

The Comforter

When we draw our last breath,
We will relax in the arms of

___ ___ ___ ___ ___.

Key Verse:
"I will not leave you comfortless: I will come to you" (John 14:18, KJV).

Scripture Reading:
Genesis 35:16-20

Ding-a-ling. "I'll get it." Melinda sang as she ran to answer the door. Since receiving the Holy Ghost, she sang all the time. As she started to open the door, a taffy ball of fur got in her way. "Move over, Buffy," she scolded.

A delivery man stood patiently waiting. "Package for Miss Melinda Larson," he said.

"Ooohhh, that's me!" Melinda squealed. As she signed for the package, Buffy squeezed between her legs and ran into the yard. Melinda carried the package into the den where Mrs. Larson was reading. "Look, Mother. This big package is for me. It's from Grandmother."

Mrs. Larson put down her book. "I imagine it's the comforter she has been making for you. Open it."

In a few quick jerks, Melinda tore the wrapping from the box. "Oh, it is! It is!" She pulled out a peach and mint-green comforter. "It's beautiful." She held it to her face. "And so soft and warm and . . . and. . . ."

Mrs. Larson finished, "And comfortable."

Melinda gathered it in her arms. "I'm going to put it on my bed right now."

She was standing back admiring her bed when a terrible screech of tires and a puppy's yelp caused her heart to catch its breath. "Oh, Mother!" she cried. "It's Buffy."

Mrs. Larson was already out the door. Melinda ran down the hall and outside. Her mother was kneeling in the middle of the street over Buffy's lifeless form.

Melinda covered her eyes and sobbed. "No! No! It can't be! Buffy can't be dead." She dropped to the porch step and sobbed uncontrollably.

She felt her mother's arms go around her. "Let's go in the house, Melinda." She pulled the girl to her feet.

That night Melinda lay huddled under her new comforter when her father came into the room. He sat down on the side of the bed. Melinda's swollen eyes peered out at him.

"I'm so sorry about Buffy, Melinda. We're going to miss him a lot," Mr. Larson said softly.

Melinda sniffed. A lump in her throat blocked her words. Mr. Larson patted her shoulder. "Your new quilt is lovely," he said. "Grandmother put a lot of work into making it. That should make you feel very loved." He leaned his head to one side. "How does it feel under there?"

Melinda grinned slightly. "Warm and soft and comfortable. I guess that's why it's called a comforter."

Mr. Larson nodded, "I know another Comforter who makes me feel very much loved."

Melinda fluffed her pillow. "Do you have a comforter?"

"Yes," her father replied. "The Holy Spirit is my Comforter. He comforts me when I'm heartbroken and sad."

Melinda's eyes widened. "That's why I felt better after I prayed," she said. "I was crying about Buffy, and it was like the Spirit of God whispered in my heart, 'Remember the good times.' So I started thinking about all the happy times we've had with B-B-Buffy, and I started to feel better. I'm still sad, but it's different. It's a kinda warm and soft feeling . . . like . . . like this comforter."

The Reason:
(Riddle answer: death)

Death is as much a part of life as breathing. We are all touched by grief at some time, whether we lose a relative, a friend, or a pet. When Rachel died, Jacob felt deep grief, but he was comforted by the baby son that God gave him.

Joseph was just a little boy when his mother, Rachel, died, leaving him with a baby brother. Think of three words that might describe Joseph's feelings.
- How does the Holy Spirit comfort us
- Do you know someone who is grieving? What can you do to comfort them? When are you going to do it?

When you are hurting, sad, and blue,
Let the Holy Spirit comfort you.

43

It Takes Time

Rearrange the letters to make the name of a tree.
REAP

___ ___ ___ ___

Key Verse:
Rest in the Lord, and wait patiently for Him (Psalm 37:7).

Scripture Reading:
Genesis 35:23-27

"Is this deep enough, Daddy?" Benny asked as he wiped the sweat from his brow with his shirt sleeve.

Mr. Moore dropped a sapling into the hole to measure it. He nodded, "I think so."

Little Kelli ran her fingers through the pile of dirt beside the hole. "I wanna help, too," she begged.

"You can help push the dirt back in the hole." Big brother Benny shoveled dirt around the little pear tree.

Kelli sprinkled dirt into the hole. "I want a pear."

Mr. Moore tousled her hair. "Then you'd better go ask your mother for one. It will be a few years before there are any pears on this tree."

Benny looked up. "How long?"

Mr. Moore rubbed his chin. "When I was a boy, we planted a pear tree. Best I can remember it took three years before it produced anything. And then it was only one pear. The next year it had a dozen or so. But the year after that, wow! We had pears everywhere."

Benny frowned. "That means it will be six or seven years before we get many pears off this tree. We aren't going to stay here that long, are we, Dad?"

Mr. Moore raised his eyebrows. "Not stay in West Fork six or seven years? Benny, we came here to build a church, remember? That's takes time."

"I know, but we've been here twelve months." Benny stomped the dirt around the sapling. "And only three people have received the Holy Ghost. At that rate, it will take years to build a church the size of the one in Pineville. I wish we'd move back there where my friends are."

Mr. Moore leaned on his shovel. "I know you get lonely, but you have a few friends here. And we have a few saints."

Kelli wiped her face with a dirty hand. "Lisa's my friend."

Mr. Moore laughed at her smudged face. "I believe the church will grow like the pear tree. A few at first, then more, and in time, an abundant crop. It takes time to build a church. God has promised to bless us in West Fork. We must work and wait for the harvest." He started far the house. "Let's wash up and I'll beat you at checkers."

Later as Mrs. Moore announced dinner, she asked, "Where's Kelli?"

Mr. Moore moved a checker into king's row. "I thought she was with you. We'll finish this after dinner," he told Benny. "Let's go find little sister."

They searched the house. No Kelli. "Check the back yard, Benny," Mrs. Moore suggested.

In a few minutes Benny came in, pulling a dirty-faced, angry little girl. "Where was she?" Mrs. Moore asked.

Benny laughed, "In the back yard watching for the pears to grow."

"That old pear tree's no good," the little girl raged.

Mr. Moore picked up the little girl and started for the bathroom.

Benny sat down at the table. "I told her some things take time, but I doubt if she got the message."

His dad looked over his shoulder and winked, "Did you?"

Benny grinned, "Yes, sir, I got the message."

The Reason:
(Riddle answer: pear)

God promised Abram that he would be the father of a great nation and possess the land where he walked. Twenty-five years later Abraham and Sarah had one son. About sixty years after that Isaac had twin sons. It was about one hundred years before it took more than ten fingers to count Abraham's family. And it was hundreds of years before Abraham's family possessed the land of Canaan.

- Name something you want that you are waiting for.
- Why do you think God sometimes makes us wait?

Remember this rhyme;
Growing takes time.

44

My Father's Favorite

What was Jacob (Israel's) occupation?

Key Verse:
Behold what manner of love the Father has bestowed on us, that we should be called children of God (I John 3:1).

Scripture Reading:
Genesis 37:1-4

Mr. Anderson stood in the shadows of the hall and listened to his children arguing in the living room.

"No, you're not. I am!" Six-year-old Brian's voice popped. "I'm the only boy."

Ten-year-old Lisa stormed, "I'm the oldest so I am."

"Not either," three-year-old Jessica declared. "Me am."

Mr. Anderson wrinkled his brow. What were they fussing about this time?

Brian snorted with disgust. "I know I'm Daddy's favorite. He takes me fishing."

"So?" Lisa countered. "Who wants to go fishing? He helps me with my homework."

"So? Who wants to do homework?" Brian snapped back.

"Daddy sits me on His lap and tells me stories," Jessica reminded them. "So he loves me the bestest."

Mr. Anderson's frown faded into a grin. They were arguing about him. Each child seemed to think he or she was his favorite. He stepped into the doorway and quietly watched the children.

Lisa pointed at Brian. "He gave you a spanking."

Brian shrugged, "So? He grounded you."

"He hugged me," Jessica sang.

"What's all the arguing about?" Father interrupted.

The children looked up in surprise. Jessica ran to him. "Lisa and Brian said you love them the bestest, but you spanked Brian and you grounded Lisa, but you just hugged me, so you love me the bestest."

With a grin Father picked up the little girl. "You're all my favorites. Brian is my favorite son. Lisa is my favorite first-born daughter, and you, Jessica, are my favorite baby girl. I love each one of my children the 'bestest,' the bestest that I possibly can."

"But you spanked Brian and grounded Lisa," Jessica reminded.

Father chuckled, "Yes, I did. And I probably will again. I corrected them because I love them."

Jessica's face fell. "Don't you love me? You never grounded me."

Father's shoulders shook. "Don't worry. Your day will come. Of course I love you."

Jessica threw her arms around her father's neck. "Know what, Daddy? You're my bestest daddy, and Mommy's my bestest mommy."

Father pulled Lisa and Brian into his arms. "I'd say we are all each other's favorites."

Lisa smiled up at her dad. "Does God have favorites?"

Father nodded. "Yes. Every one of us is His favorite. We are all special to Him."

As Jessica wiggled out of her father's arms, she said, "I guess God loves us the very bestest that He can."

The Reason:

(Riddle answer: He was a painter, because he gave Joseph "a coat of many colors.")

It is a wonderful feeling to be loved, to be someone's favorite. Never forget that you are God's favorite child.
- Who was Israel's (Jacob's) favorite son?
- Why? How did Israel show his partiality?
- Name someone who loves you "bestest" (the best they can)?

In this we can boast,
God loves each the most.

45

𝒟anny's 𝒟ream

What animal frightens children in their sleep?

Key Verse:
Delight yourself also in the Lord, and He shall give you the desires of your heart (Psalm 37:4).

Scripture Reading:
Genesis 37:5-11

Vrrrooommm. Danny gunned the motor as he swerved his cycle to miss a giant python that lay curled in the middle of the jungle path. Lifting the handlebars he sailed over a fallen log. Monkeys scolded from their hiding places. In the distance he could hear the roar of the flooded river.

"Dear Jesus, help me get across," he prayed. "I have to take the gospel to the lost tribe of Whatchenee. They are waiting. . . ."

"Danny, I asked you a question." Miss Williams's stern voice shocked him out of his dream world.

Danny blinked his glazed eyes and looked around him. What a letdown! The future was the present, the cycle a desk, and the jungle Bethany Christian School. Monkeys weren't scolding him, but Miss Williams was.

"You were daydreaming again, Danny." She put a hand on the boy's shoulder. "Have you finished your English?"

Danny's shoulders sagged. He shook his head. "I don't know why I have to learn English and grammar and all that stuff," he said. "I need to be studying the language they speak in Africa."

"Africa?" Miss Williams echoed. "Why Africa?"

A dreamy look crossed Danny's face. "Because I'm going to be a missionary to Africa." He waited for His teacher to laugh, but she didn't.

"Really? That's wonderful," she replied. She pulled up a chair and sat down beside the boy. "Did you know that many people in Africa speak English?"

Danny's eyebrows lifted. "Really?"

Miss Williams nodded. "Really. And in order to learn the other languages they speak, you need a good basic knowledge of English."

Danny looked skeptical. "You just want me to finish my schoolwork."

Miss Williams grinned. "Yes, I do." She sobered, "But I am telling you the truth. Why do you want to be a missionary, Danny?"

Danny looked thoughtful. "Well . . . I . . . I feel like it is what the Lord wants me to do. And I . . . I . . . I want to please Him. Ever since I was a little boy," said the ten-year-old boy, "I've wanted to be a missionary in Africa."

"It's your dream," Miss Williams said.

"My dream?" Danny repeated. "No, I didn't dream it. I just felt it."

"I didn't mean a sleepy-time dream," Miss Williams explained. "I mean a vision, a goal, and a plan for the future."

Danny nodded. "Yeah, that's it. It's my goal, what I want to be when I grow up."

Miss Williams stood up. "Do you know how to make that dream come true, Danny?" she asked.

He shrugged, "Just wait and hope, I guess."

"No," his teacher said. "You won't reach your goal by daydreaming. To make dreams come true, you must work. In order to be a missionary in Africa, you must have a good education. . . ."

Danny groaned. "I knew it was coming."

As Miss Williams turned to leave, he grinned, "Maybe I should take motorcycle driving lessons."

"What?" Miss Williams stopped and looked over her shoulder. "Motorcycle driving lessons? Whatever for?"

"To make my dream come true," Danny chuckled as he started to work on his English lesson.

The Reason:

(Riddle answer: night-mare)

God gave Joseph two dreams which promised him a great future. Many people laughed at Joseph's dreams and doubted they would ever come true. But Joseph held onto his dreams, even when everything went wrong. (But that's getting ahead of the story.)

- What is your dream? What are you doing to make that dream come true?
- Is daydreaming good or bad (or both)? Explain.

Dreams come true
When you work them through.

46

The Teacher's Pet

For how many pieces of gold did Joseph's brothers sell him?

Key Verse:
Jealousy [is] as cruel as the grave (Song of Solomon 8:6).

Scripture Reading:
Genesis 37:12-36

After Sunday school Brock gathered his pals around him. "My dad said he'd take me and my buddies fishing next Saturday. Who wants to go?"

"We all do," Kevin replied. "Is Casey going, too?"

Brock rolled his eyes at the boy standing alone across the church. "Naw. He wouldn't enjoy it. He's a better singer than fisherman." The boys snickered. "We can do without the teacher's pet," Brock continued.

"Yeah," Nelson sneered. "Casey-boy gets the lead in everything. Just because I lost my part last time and Kevin forgot to come to practice and you went out of town. . . ."

Brock interrupted, "That's no reason to give Casey the lead every time. He's not the only one who can sing." The others nodded agreement. "Gotta go," Brock said. "My mom's eyeing me."

That afternoon Brock was playing with Rusty and Rover in the back yard when Uncle Jason came through the gate carrying a coal-black puppy.

With Rusty and Rover at his heels, Brock ran to meet his uncle. Uncle Jason rolled the ball of fur into Brock's arms. "Oh, can I have him? Please?"

Rusty and Rover sniffed and stiffened. Rusty bared his teeth, and Rover growled deep in his throat.

Uncle Jason grinned. "If your folks and these two mutts," he pointed at the other dogs, "will let you."

Brock ran for the house with the pup hugged under his chin. "Mother and Dad will love this teddy bear."

A couple hours later Brock carried Maxwell, the new pup, into the back yard. Setting Max down beside him, he poured food into the dogs' bowls. "Rusty! Rover! Come meet your new friend," he invited.

"Brock!" Mrs. Taylor called from the house. "Telephone. It's Casey."

Brock curled his nose. "Coming," he called. Under his breath he muttered, "Wonder what the teacher's pet wants? Probably wants to go fishing with us."

Inside he picked up the receiver. "Hello . . . Yeah . . . Ye. . . ." A terrible commotion in the back yard drowned out his words. "Brock! Come quick!" Mrs. Taylor yelled. "Rusty and Rover have attacked your pup."

"Call you back," Brock screamed as he dropped the phone.

Mrs. Taylor was there ahead of him, beating off the big dogs. The little pup lay panting and whining on the ground. Gently, Brock picked him up. "Poor baby," he crooned.

Mrs. Taylor ran her hands through the pup's fur. "He doesn't seem to be hurt. He's just scared."

Brock turned to the big dogs who were cowering in the corner of the yard. "Shame on you! Why did you attack Max?"

"They were jealous," Mrs. Taylor answered for the dogs. "They don't want to share their yard and food. Jealousy makes dogs and people do mean things."

Brock looked at the dogs through narrowed eyes. "Well, they'd better learn to share. Max is here to stay!"

Carrying the shaking pup, Brock followed his mother into the house. Seeing the dangling telephone, he remembered, "Oh, I've got to call Casey." Brock looked at the pup huddled in his arms. His face softened. A feeling of shame crossed his heart as his mother's words soaked in. *Jealousy makes dogs—and people—do mean things.*

Brock gulped. "I . . . I . . . I need to ask Casey if he wants to go fishing with us next Saturday."

The Reason:

(Riddle answer: None. They sold him for twenty pieces of silver.)

Jealousy caused Joseph's brothers to do something they regretted for the rest of their lives. Jealousy is cruel. Don't let it get a grip on you.
- Why were Joseph's brothers jealous of him?
- Are you jealous of anyone? Why? (Look deep in your heart and be honest.) If so, ask God to cleanse you before you do something you will always regret.

Before jealousy makes you mean,
Ask God to make you clean.

What animal cannot tell a lie?

47

Not Guilty

What animal cannot tell a lie?

Key Verse:
Having a good conscience, that when they defame you as evildoers . . . [they] may be ashamed (I Peter 3:16).

Scripture Reading:
Genesis 39:1-20

"Hey, kid, come here. I want to talk to you." Big John leaned over the counter and pointed at Tommy.

Tommy stared in amazement. "Me? Me, sir?"

"You're the only one in here, ain't ya?" growled the clerk. "I saw you yesterday when you took that candy."

Tommy's eyes widened. "Me? Me, sir?"

"Yeah, you! You stuffed your pockets full of candy, 'bout five dollars' worth, I'd say." Big John's eyes narrowed. "You pay for it and we'll just forget about it."

Tommy protested, "But, sir, I didn't do it."

The clerk grabbed the boy's arm. "Don't feed me that line. Pay up right now or I'll call the police."

Fear grabbed Tommy's stomach. "But I didn't! I didn't! Besides I don't have five dollars."

"Then you just run home and get it. And don't you tell nobody what you're doing neither, or the police'll be after you in a minute," Big John threatened.

Half blinded by tears Tommy ran from the store and down the street.

Kurwhump! "Ooops! Better watch it, son . . . Why, Tommy, what's the matter?"

Tommy looked up into the face of his teacher. He caught his breath in a sob. "Oh, Mr. Beasley, I . . . I . . . I guess I just wasn't watching where I was going."

Mr. Beasley examined Tommy's tear-stained face. "What's wrong, son?"

"Nothing . . . I . . . I . . . Oh, Mr. Beasley," Tommy's shoulders shook as he poured out the story of Big John's accusation.

Mr. Beasley's expression grew dark as he listened. "Tommy, you are one of the most honest boys I know. You would never shoplift." As he took the boy's hand, he chuckled, "Five dollars' worth of candy in your pockets? Must have pretty big pockets in those jeans." He led him back to the store.

Big John swallowed twice when they entered. He scowled at Tommy. "I told you . . . I mean. . . ."

"Yes? What did you tell him?" Mr. Beasley asked. Big John didn't answer. After a brief pause, Mr. Beasley continued, "What time was it when Tommy took that candy?"

"Uhhhh, i-i-it was right after school. Yeah, right after school yesterday," Big John stuttered.

"But that couldn't be," Mr. Beasley replied. "Tommy went on a field trip yesterday. He didn't get back until six."

Big John's face turned red. "Then it must have been the day before yesterday. Yeah, that's when it was."

Mr. Beasley shook his head. "No. Tommy's not guilty. He did not steal one piece of candy."

Big John clinched his teeth. "How do you know?"

"I know because I know Tommy," Mr. Beasley replied. "He is not a thief. Last week he turned in a dollar he found on the playground." He looked the clerk straight in the eye. "How many innocent kids have you tricked into paying you off so you wouldn't call the police?" he asked bluntly.

"Tommy's the fir . . . I mean . . . who are you to question me?"

Mr. Beasley placed a hand on Tommy's shoulder. "It would be a good idea if he's also the last. Let's go, Tommy."

Outside Tommy smiled, "Thank you, Mr. Beasley."

Mr. Beasley squeezed the boy's shoulder. "And thank you, Tommy, for being a boy someone can trust. We need more like you."

The Reason:

(Riddle answer: No animal can tell a lie. Animals cannot talk.)

There was no one to stand up for Joseph, but God knew the truth. And God remembered.

Because Joseph refused to do wrong, he was lied about and thrown in prison.
- Think of three words to describe how you would have felt in his place.
- Has anyone ever told a lie about you? What did you do about it?

No matter what others say,
Be true to God every day.

The Test of the Best

What kind of dog can tell time?

Key Verse:
Well done, good and faithful servant; you were faithful over a few things, I will make you ruler over many things (Matthew 25:21).

Scripture Reading:
Genesis 39:20-23

"Do you know the memory verse, Lisa?" Miss Cindy asked.

Lisa stared at her shoes. "I . . . I think I do," she stammered. She took a deep breath. "Well done, g, g, g . . . good and . . . and faithful servant; you were . . . ahhhhhh"

"Faithful," filled in her cousin Mindi.

Lisa's face turned red. "Faithful . . . ahhhhh . . . faithful over a few things, I will make you . . . ahhhh . . . make you. . . ."

"Ruler over many things," Mindi finished.

Lisa boiled. "Thanks for the help, Mindi, but I can do without it!"

Mindi looked shocked. "But you didn't know the verse."

Lisa resented her cousin. It was an ugly feeling she didn't like, but she couldn't seem to help it. Mindi was everything Lisa was not: smart, pretty, popular.

"We missed you yesterday, Mindi," Miss Cindy said. "We had a good time passing out revival handbills."

Mindi straightened her collar. "I forgot."

"Yeah," remarked Paul, "like you forgot last month when we raked Mr. Brown's yard. You always forget the work projects, Mindi, but never the parties."

Mindi wrinkled her nose at Paul. Everyone knew she liked him.

Miss Cindi glanced at the clock. "Next Sunday we will elect officers for our service club. Class dismissed."

After church Lisa and her parents went home with Mindi's family. When dinner was over Mrs. Clark asked, "Would you girls please do the dishes?"

Ignoring Mindi's scowl Lisa answered, "Sure, Aunt Jo."

Later Mrs. Clark came into the kitchen. "Where's Mindi?"

Lisa shrugged. "I think she's in the back yard playing with Princess."

Aunt Jo rolled her eyes. "That girl! I can't depend on her for anything." She picked up a dishcloth. "Are you going to enter Pudge in the dog show at the mall, Lisa?"

"Pudge?" Lisa asked in surprise. "My Pudge? But he's just a mutt. I can't enter him in the dog show."

"He's the most obedient mutt I ever saw," Aunt Jo said. "You should enter him. Obedience is a big factor in winning."

When Lisa mentioned entering her dog in the show, Mindi laughed, "You're wasting your time. I'm going to enter Princess. She has a pedigree."

Aunt Jo glanced at her daughter. "She also has the nastiest temper I ever saw in a dog."

Lisa noticed that Mindi wasn't laughing the next Saturday when Pudge was awarded the prize for being "The Best of the Show" while Princess tugged at her leash and growled.

Nor was Mindi laughing the next morning when Lisa was elected secretary of the service club.

"I don't know why they elected you," Mindi whispered. "You can't even spell."

Lisa grinned, "I know, but I do have a good memory. I can remember when we have a project going. I can even remember last Sunday's memory verse. 'Well done, good and faithful servant: you were faithful over a few things, I will make you ruler over many things.'"

The Reason:

(Riddle answer: a watchdog)

Joseph dreamed of being a ruler. Instead, he became a slave. So he decided to be the best slave he could possibly be. And he became a ruler over the slaves. Then he became a prisoner. So guess what? He became the best prisoner he could be, and he became a ruler over the prisoners.

- Why do you think God allowed Joseph to be sold into slavery and put in prison?
- What is faithfulness? Why is it important?
- Name some ways in which you can be faithful.

To be blessed, do your best.

49

Part-Time Help

Cross all the Xs, Ys, and Zs to find what Pharoah's butler forgot.
XJYZXOSZYXEXZPZYXHXX

Key Verse:
A friend loves at all times (Proverbs 17:17).

Scripture Reading:
Genesis 40:1-23

"Mother! Pray! Pray!" Heather screamed as she ran into the house with blood dripping from her finger.

Mrs. Blake came running. "What happened?"

"I cut my finger on a piece of glass," Heather wailed. "Pray, Mother, pray! I don't want to get stitches."

Mrs. Blake carried Heather into the bathroom. As she examined the hurt finger, she prayed, "Jesus, help us." When the blood was washed away, Heather's sobs quietened. "It's not deep, honey." Mrs. Blake put a bandaid on the cut.

Soon the injury was forgotten, and the little girl was back outside jumping the rope with her friend Jocelyn.

Later Mrs. Blake called, "Heather, come in. It's time to get ready for church."

Angrily, Heather threw down the rope. "Always when I'm having fun, I have to quit and go to church."

Jocelyn grimaced. "My family only goes on Sunday mornings." She waved over her shoulder. "See you tomorrow."

As Heather started down the hall, she complained, "I don't see why we have to go to church all the time. Why can't we just go on Sunday mornings like Jocelyn's family?"

Before Mrs. Blake could reply, Heather's big sister burst out of the bedroom. Seeing Alicia's stormy face, Heather asked, "What are you mad about?"

"My job!" Alicia raged. "They always want me to work when I need off and don't want me when I can work."

Mrs. Blake pushed Heather toward the bathroom. "I take it Mr. Dawson needs you to work Saturday?"

"Of course!" Alicia's face crumpled. "Now I won't get to go with my teen class to the lake. Last Saturday when there wasn't anything to do, Mr. Dawson didn't need me."

Mrs. Blake followed Heather into the bathroom and began brushing her hair. In the mirror, Heather saw Alicia leaning against the door frame, her eyes filled with tears. "That's the hazard of a part-time job," Mrs. Blake reminded. "You knew it would be that way."

Heather put a hand to her hair. "Ouch! That pulled."

"Sorry!" Mrs. Blake muttered.

Heather glanced at her sister's reflection in the mirror. "I think Mr. Dawson's selfish," she sympathized. "He doesn't care what Alicia wants to do. It's just what he needs."

"That's Mr. Dawson's right. He's the employer," Mrs. Blake stated as she pulled Heather's hair into a rubber band. "But you have no right to treat God that way."

Heather's look met her mother's in the mirror. "Me?"

Mrs. Blake nodded. "Yes, you. You want God to be your part-time help. You want Him when you need Him . . . like when you cut your finger . . . or get scared in the dark. But when everything is going okay and you don't need anything, you want to forget Him. You don't want to go to His house. . . ."

"Look at the time," Alicia put in. "We'd better hurry or we'll be late for church." She made a dash for the bedroom.

As Heather brushed her teeth, she noticed the band-aid on her finger. "Thank You, Jesus," she sputtered, "for helping me all the time."

The Reason:

(Riddle answer: Joseph)

When the butler's troubles were over, he promptly forgot Joseph. Only when he needed help again did he remember the young man in prison.

- How do you think Joseph felt when he realized the butler had forgotten him? How would you have felt?
- Have you ever been forgotten? How did you feel?
- Is the Lord Jesus your full-time friend, or do you call on Him only when you need Him?

On you can Jesus depend?
Are you His full- or part-time friend?

50

Forgotten

Pharaoh's butler remembered something everyone would like to forget. What was it?

Take Joseph from the prison to the palace, picking up letters as you go, to find what it was.

___ ___ ___ ___ ___ ___ ___

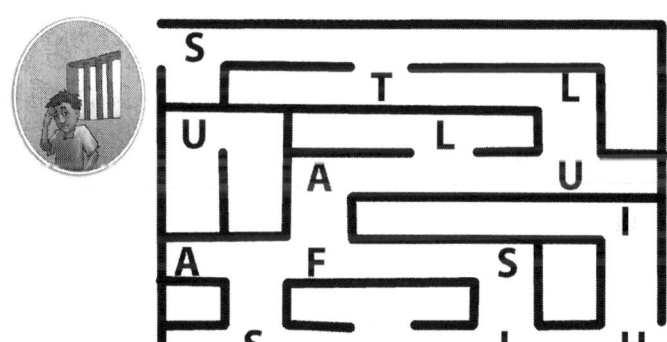

Key Verse:
"Forgive, and you will be forgiven" (Luke 6:37).

Scripture Reading:
Genesis 41:1-13

Sandy's freckles were popping as she slammed the car door. "Bridgette wasn't home!" she told her parents. "She promised she'd come to Sunday school to help me win the contest. And this is the last Sunday."

Mr. Walker pulled the car away from the curb. "Maybe her folks decided to go out of town," he said.

"She could have called me," Sandy raged.

"Perhaps she forgot," suggested Mrs. Walker." Ask her again next week."

Sandy straightened her shoulders. "I will not. This is the last Sunday of the contest. Anyway, why ask her if she can't remember to come?"

Beside Sandy, Tim groaned, "Mom, my head hurts."

Mrs. Walker glanced over her shoulder at the boy's flushed face. "I hope you don't have fever!" she exclaimed.

But he did. By the next morning, Tim was very sick. As Sandy left for school, he asked, "Will you get my homework from Mrs. Brown, Sandy?"

"Sure," Sandy promised as she grabbed her books and ran to meet the bus.

As Sandy boarded the bus, Bridgette called, "I've saved you a seat."

Sandy glared at the girl but accepted the seat. For several minutes Bridgette chattered happily, and then she peered at her friend. "What's the matter with you?" she asked.

Sandy snorted, "Don't you know?"

Bridgette looked blank. "No. How could I?"

"You promised to go to church with me yesterday. We drove across town to get you and you weren't even home!" Sandy turned her back on her friend. "And I lost the Sunday school contest because you didn't come."

Bridgette's mouth fell open. "I forgot. I'm sorry, Sandy."

Sandy didn't answer. So Bridgette turned her back, too. They didn't speak to each other all day. On the way home that afternoon, Bridgette sat in the front of the bus and Sandy sat in the back.

At home Sandy dropped her books on the couch. From the recliner Tim asked, "Where's my homework?"

Sandy's hand flew to her mouth. "I forgot. I'm sorry." Even as she said the words, in her mind Sandy heard Bridgette's voice, *I forgot. I'm sorry.*

Tim shrugged and gave her a lopsided grin. "Well, if I don't have it, I can't do it, can I? Guess I'll just have to play catch-up later."

Sandy squeezed her brother's shoulder as she passed him. "You're a swell guy, Tim. I'm glad you're my brother."

Tim stared in amazement. "What did you say?"

As Sandy dialed the phone, she grinned, "I forgot. My memory's pretty short these days." She jerked her attention back to the phone. "Hello? Bridgette? Bridgette, about yesterday . . . I'm sorry I was so hateful. Could you go to Sunday school with me next Sunday? . . . Oh, the contest is over. I'd just like you to go with me . . . Great. I'll see you in the morning. Save me a seat on the bus. OK?"

The Reason:
(Riddle answer: his faults)

Two years passed before the butler remembered Joseph. For Joseph that meant two more long years in prison. Not much fun!

- Have you ever forgotten to keep a promise? What did you do about it when you remembered?
- Has anyone ever broken a promise he or she made to you? How do you feel toward that person?
- How do you know God keeps His promises?

Forgive those who forget.

51

The Promotion

What is the most important ability you can have?

Key Verse:
For exaltation comes neither from the east nor from the west nor from the south. But God is the Judge: He puts down one and exalts another' (Psalm 75:6-7).

Scripture Reading:
Genesis 41:14-16, 25-44

As the Collins family emerged from the house, Steve said, "Boy, the Chevy is looking neat, Dad. Let's go to church in it this morning."

Mr. Collins looked at the car he was restoring. "I don't know," he hesitated. "It looks great on the outside, but I've a lot of work to do under the hood yet."

"Please, Dad?" Steve begged. "I've been telling the guys about our classic, and they're dying to see it."

"Well, okay," Mr. Collins relented. "We'll chance it."

As they neared the church, Mrs. Collins asked, "Do you know your memory verse, Steve?"

Steve muttered, "No. I didn't have time to learn it."

Mrs. Collins frowned, "Did you do your report on Joseph?"

Steve stared out the window. "No. I said I was busy. I don't think Mr. Reynolds ought to give us homework for Sunday school. We get enough of that at school!"

Later in class Steve listened with interest as Mr. Reynolds announced, "Pastor Hall has asked me to choose two boys from this class to serve as junior ushers for the youth revival."

Steve straightened his tie as he ran an appraising eye over his classmates. *Not much competition here,* he thought. He felt sure he would be chosen. After all, his dad was on the church board, his mother was the secretary, and he was the best-looking, sharpest-dressed guy in the junior class. And, of course, he never missed church.

Mr. Reynolds continued, "So I have chosen Mark and Bob."

Mark? Steve couldn't believe his ears. He had figured Bob would be one, but Mark? Why, he didn't even own a suit.

"Now, Steve, if you're ready, we'd like to hear your report on Joseph," Mr. Reynolds smiled at the boy.

Steve's face turned red. "Ahhhh . . . I . . . I didn't get it. I . . . uhhhh . . . I've been busy helping my dad work on the car he's restoring."

Mr. Reynolds nodded. "Do you have your report, Mark?"

"Yes, sir," Mark replied.

On the way home from church, Steve poured out his anger. "I should have been chosen to be junior usher."

Mrs. Collins raised her eyebrows. "Oh? Why?"

Steve leaned over the front seat. "Because I'm . . . I'm . . . I'm your son."

Mr. Collins frowned, "So what?"

"So what?" Steve echoed. "We're an important family in this church. Besides I'm the best loo . . . I mean, I dress neater than Mark. What will visitors think when the usher isn't even wearing a suit?"

"What will they think?" asked Mrs. Collins quietly.

"Why, they'll think . . . they'll think that we're a . . . a sloppy bunch of people," Steve stuttered. "Besides I'm always at church."

Mrs. Collins looked at her son. "True, you're always there, even if you are pouting and angry because we made you go. I wonder if you. . . ."

Sputtt-s-puttt. "Oh, no," Mr. Collins muttered. "I was afraid of this." He pulled the dying car to the shoulder.

As Mr. Collins tinkered with wires under the hood, Mrs. Collins turned to Steve. "Son, it is better to ride in an ordinary car that you can depend on than a sharp-looking one that is not reliable. Dependability is mighty important. Think about it."

The Reason:

(Riddle answer: dependability)

Joseph went through a lot of tests before God promoted him to a position of honor in Egypt. Joseph had proven that he was dependable. God is not looking for smart, good-looking kids. He is looking for dependable ones.

- Why do you think Mark was chosen for junior usher instead of Steve?
- Why is it important to do small, ordinary jobs well?
- When you are given a job, can you be depended upon to finish it?

Important jobs go to the worker, not the shirker.

52

Planning Ahead

What insect is like your mother's sister?

Key Verse:
Go to the ant, you sluggard! Consider her ways and be wise (Proverbs 6:6).

Scripture Reading:
Genesis 41:46-57

"Are you learning your A-B-C's, Andrew?" Allison asked her twin as she pulled a study sheet from her Bible.

Andrew looked up. "Naw. Why should I?"

"Pastor Wise says it is important that we hide the Word of God in our hearts; that's why he asked us to learn a verse for every letter of the alphabet," Allison reminded.

But Andrew wasn't listening. He was chuckling at a joke in the comic book he was reading.

Allison quoted, "A. 'Ask, and it shall be given you. . . .'"

Andrew perked up. "Sounds like a good idea. Would you loan me a quarter, Sis?"

She frowned at her twin. "No. You get the same allowance I do. What do you do with your money?"

Andrew dropped the comic book and straddled the arm of the couch. "Spend it. That's what it's for."

"You spend it all right... on junk, comic books, Cokes, and candy. You need to learn to save," Allison scolded. "I've saved enough for a plane ticket to Grandmother Anderson's."

"Really?" Andrew looked impressed. "Maybe Dad will loan me some money. Or give me a ticket for a birthday present."

"I doubt it. Money's pretty tight around here."

"It wouldn't be if Dad didn't give every spare penny to the church or put it in savings," Andrew complained.

Mrs. Anderson came into the room as he was speaking. "Someday you'll be glad he did. It's for your education."

Andrew curled his nose. "I don't want to go to college. I'm going to get a job and earn lots of money."

"Not if you don't go to college," Allison reminded.

Andrew ignored her. "Mom, do you think Dad would loan me the money for a ticket so I can go to Grandmother's, too?"

Mrs. Anderson held out a basket to her son. "We don't have it. Go pick the cucumbers, please, Andy."

Andrew scowled. "But there's money in savings. Dad could loan it to me. I'd pay it back, a little each week."

"You know how your Father feels about borrowing money, and he will not touch your educational funds."

She pushed the basket into Andrew's hand. "Now go pick cucumbers."

Reluctantly, Andrew took the basket. "I thought when we moved to the farm, I'd spend my summer vacation riding horses, swimming in the creek, and hiking," he grumbled. "Instead I pick cucumbers, hoe corn, and snap peas. Yuck! I'm wasting my vacation. I don't even like cucumbers."

"But you love pickles," his sister reminded.

"Pickles? What have pickles got to do with cucumbers?"

Allison giggled, "He doesn't know pickles are made from cucumbers. Dumb city boy!"

Emphasizing each word, Mrs. Anderson said, "Go pick the cucumbers, Andrew." As Andrew put on his shoes, Mother asked, "What are you doing, Allison?"

"Studying my A-B-C's. I've learned up to G." She quoted, "'Go to the ant, thou sluggard; consider her ways. . . .'"

Andrew looked up from tying his shoe. He interrupted, "That's a funny verse. Who wants to go to the ant?"

Mrs. Anderson tapped his shoulder. "You could learn a lot from the ant, Son. Ants work hard in the summer and store up food so they can survive in the winter. They plan for the future, like we save for your education."

"That's why we memorize Bible verses, too," Allison reasoned. "We're storing them up for when we need them."

Andrew shook his jeans leg. "Yeah, that's why I pick cucumbers, too." As he left the room, he asked with a grin, "Wonder if ants like pickles?"

The Reason:

(Riddle answer: ant/aunt)

The Lord warned Pharaoh of the coming famine, and He gave Joseph the plan to prepare for the future.
- What was Joseph's plan to prepare for the famine?
- How can memorizing Bible verses prepare you for the future?
- What can an ant teach people?

Learn from the ant;
Don't say can't.

53

Dreams Come True

"Bow down before that kid?
Never," we said. But we did.
Who were we?

Key Verse:
Delight yourself also in the LORD, and He shall give you the desires of your heart (Psalm 37:4).

Scripture Reading:
Genesis 42:1-6

Ivan glued his gaze on the man behind the pulpit. He didn't even notice when Justin poked him in the ribs.

"It seems like yesterday I sat where you are sitting," the missionary said. "Actually, it was fifteen years ago that I was a student here at Bethany Christian School."

Missionary Daniel West turned to a lady sitting on the platform behind him. "Do you remember how I daydreamed in class, Sister Williams?" he asked.

The gray-haired lady laughed, "I certainly do."

Brother West turned back to the students. "I remember one day especially," he said. "I was daydreaming about riding a motorcycle through the jungles. I thought I heard monkeys chattering. Instead, Sister Williams was scolding me for not paying attention. Do boys still daydream in class?"

Ivan felt his face redden as the teacher answered, "They certainly do." He knew she was thinking about yesterday when she had scolded him for daydreaming and not finishing his math. He hated math!

Brother West continued, "I am living proof that dreams can come true. If there is something you want to be for God, something you want to do for Him, you can be it . . . you can do it."

Yeah, that's easy for you to say. You don't understand, Ivan argued silently. *I am sure your dad was a preacher, not in prison like mine.*

The missionary's words cut into Ivan's thoughts. "As long as I can remember, I dreamed of being a missionary. Thanks to Sister Williams, I wasn't allowed to simply dream. She put me to work."

Beside Ivan, Justin snorted, but Ivan ignored him. He had to hear every word. No one knew . . . no one . . . Ivan's dream of being a missionary pilot. But Brother West looked right at him, as if he knew.

"My parents abandoned me when I was five," he said.

Ivan leaned forward. *Maybe this guy does understand,* he thought. *But he's smart. He doesn't stutter like me.*

"I was pushed from one foster home to another," the missionary continued, "and labeled as retarded. When I was eleven and still in the third grade, I was placed in a Pentecostal home. My foster parents enrolled me in this school. And God, helped by Sister Williams, took control of my life." He winked at the teacher.

"It won't always be easy, but dreams can come true. It takes prayer, patience, and hard work. It won't happen overnight. It may take years, but you can be whatever you want to be for God. You can do whatever you dream of doing for Him, if you work at it. Let's pray."

As the missionary prayed, Ivan exhaled. A vision of the instrument panel of an airplane flashed behind his closed eyelids. It seemed to be magnified. There were numbers everywhere. Ivan squeezed his eyelids tighter. The numbers grew larger. Every gauge was filled with numbers. He gulped.

"Give each child here the self-discipline and determination to make their dreams come true," Brother West prayed. "In Jesus' name and for His glory. Amen."

Ivan opened his eyes. The missionary was looking straight at him. Through the noise, Ivan read Brother West's lips. "Go for it, son. You can do it."

Ivan grinned and picked up his math book. He held it high over his head in a symbol of victory. He didn't see his teacher smile through her tears as he ran from the room.

The Reason:

(Riddle answer: Joseph's brothers)

It was at least thirteen years before Joseph's dreams came true.
- Name some things Joseph suffered during this time.
- Why was it important for Ivan to learn math? How is your school work important to making your dreams come true?
- Where does God fit into your plans for the future?

Dreams Come True

Remember: dreams come true,
When you work them through.

54

Caught!

What is the heaviest thing you can carry?

Key Verse:
"Be sure your sin will find you out" (Numbers 32:23).

Scripture Reading:
Genesis 42:21-38

Glen's feet hardly touched the pavement. He burst into the house. "I've got a job," he panted.

Grandmother Thomas met him in the hall. "Doing what?"

"Delivering sale bills for Holmes's Hardware," Glen gasped. "Mr. Holmes is going to pay me three cents for every sale bill I deliver. He gave me five hundred for Eastbrook Estates," Glen pointed at the bag beside him. "He said I could have more tomorrow if I do a good job today."

"Five hundred?" repeated Grandfather Thomas. "That'll take a while."

"I've got all day. Well, all afternoon."

"Uncle Melvin and Aunt Lou are coming tonight," Grandmother reminded.

"I'll be finished by supper," Glen assured her. "Got any lunch meat? I'll make a sandwich and get started."

Soon Glen was hard at work. The houses in Eastbrook were scattered. "Could get rid of these a lot faster at Briarwood Apartments," Glen muttered as he wiped the sweat from his brow. He hadn't realized it was so hot, but they needed the money. Glen knew his grandparents stretched every penny to provide for him.

He glanced at his watch. It was later than he thought . . . and hotter than he thought . . . and harder than he thought. He shifted the bag to his other arm. He still had a hundred or so. A trash dumpster stood at the corner of Lakewood and Thirty-first. *I could just dump these and no one would ever know. Grandmother will be worrying about me. Uncle Melvin's coming,* he reasoned.

Glen looked in all directions. No one was in sight. Quickly, he slipped the bag into the dumpster.

When he opened the front door, an eerie silence met him. Then he heard a faint sob. He ran into the living room. Grandmother sat with her face hid in her apron. Grandfather knelt beside her. His face was gray.

"What's wrong?" Glen asked.

Grandfather took a deep breath. "Melvin. . . . ," he stopped and started over. "Your Uncle Melvin's been arrested."

Glen jerked to attention. "Arrested? What for?"

Grandmother looked up. "For being AWOL."

"AWOL?" Glen echoed. "Absent without leave? But Uncle Melvin's not in the army."

Grandfather stood up. "Not now. But he was six years ago. He didn't like it so he just walked off."

Grandmother wiped her face with her apron. "We told him to turn himself in, but he wouldn't listen. He thought they had forgotten him."

"'Be sure your sins will find you out,'" Grandfather quoted. "I remember once when I was a boy, my dad sent me to plant beans. I wanted to go swimmin' so I just dumped the seeds in a hole at the end of the garden and covered them. Then I went swimmin'. I got by with it, too . . . for a couple of weeks . . . until the beans started comin' up."

Glen took a deep breath and closed his eyes. When he opened them, Grandfather was staring at him. "You okay, son?"

Glen nodded. "I . . . uhhhh . . . I'm not quite through with my job, Gramps. I'll be back in about an hour."

As he ran far the corner of Lakewood and Thirty-first, Glen prayed. "Lord, please, don't let anyone find my sins before I get there."

The Reason:
(Riddle answer: a guilty conscience)

Joseph's brothers thought their sin was covered, but they never forgot. Always their conscience nagged at them. Every time anything went wrong, they said, "It's because of what we did to Joseph."
- How does it feel to have a guilty conscience?
- How can someone get rid of a guilty conscience?
- Are there hidden sins in your life for which you need to repent? Do it now.

You can't do wrong and get by,
No matter how hard you may try.

The Checker Game

55

Can you say this tongue twister six times without stopping?

"Sin-sick souls seek a soul-saving Savior."

Key Verse:
For who has known the mind of the Lord? Or who has become His counselor? (Romans 11:34).

Scripture Reading:
Genesis 43:1-17, 26-34

Amber stared out the car window in disgust at the graying, wrinkled building slumped on the corner lot. It was the first time she had seen New Life Center. Ha! That was a joke. New Life Center looked like it was drawing its last breath. She couldn't believe her father had given up the beautiful new church in Cleveland that was packed with people every service to pastor this . . . this dump.

Apparently, her brother John was thinking the same thing for he said, "You mean we left Cleveland for this?"

Somberly, Pastor Bennett nodded.

"But why?" Amber asked.

"Because the Lord moved us here," Mrs. Bennett answered.

He did not, Amber argued silently. *Daddy and North American Van Lines did.* But she knew better than to say so.

"But, Dad," John questioned, "why would God move you here to pastor a half-dozen people when there are three hundred in Cleveland who need you? It doesn't make sense."

Pastor Bennett started the car. "'Who has known the mind of the Lord? or who has become his counselor?'" he quoted. "Someday we will understand."

Mrs. Bennett put her hand over her husband's. "I, for one, am glad to be in Del City. We are right in the center of the will of God, and that's the best place in the world to be. Now let's go find a restaurant."

Later that evening Pastor Bennett threw an empty packing box on top of a growing stack. "Enough for one day," he declared. "Does anyone know where the checkers are?"

Amber ran for the hall closet. "I just unpacked them. I'm red, Dad. You're black."

Soon they were fighting their way toward king's row. "Got ya!" Amber sang as she jumped one of her dad's men.

He groaned. "I should have seen that." As he studied the board, he asked, "What would you do if one of these checkers looked up at you and said, 'I don't like the way you're moving me, Amber. Move me over there instead of here'?"

Amber giggled. "I'd have a heart attack!"

"Me, too," her dad agreed. "Yet we often say to God, 'Why are You moving me here or there? Doing this and that in my life?'" Amber looked at the floor as Pastor Bennett continued, "We're not the only ones on the board, honey. God has a master plan for His church. We are only a small part of it. The goal is not to promote me to great glory. The goal is to win . . . to win the lost."

"Yeah, and I guess a soul in Del City is as important as one in Cleveland," John said as he joined the conversation. "And you are a good carpenter, Dad. New Life Center sure could use some help there."

"Aha!" Amber cried as her king jumped her dad's last two men. "The game's over. I won. You should have paid attention, Dad."

Pastor Bennett stood and stretched. "One move a day is about all I can manage," he laughed. He gave his daughter a bear hug. "Remember the rule."

Amber grinned, "I know. The winner puts the game up." As she gathered up the pieces, she added, "I think we're all going to be winners in Del City."

The Reason:

God moved Joseph into many strange places before he reached "king's row." Now Joseph was moving his brothers in ways that frightened them. Before he revealed himself, he wanted to know if they were the same wicked men he had known or if they had changed.
- Why do you think Joseph wanted to know this?
- How do you think Joseph felt when he saw Benjamin?
- Has there ever been a time in your life when you questioned God?

Don't question God's plan;
Just hold to His hand.

56

The Substitute

Like my brother, I was my father's favorite son;
Like my brother, I was accused of a crime I had not done.
One brother would not let another go until he saw my face.
Yet another brother offered to take my place.
What's my name?

___ ___ ___ ___ ___ ___ ___ ___

Key Verse:
Greater love has no one than this, than to lay down one's life for his friends (John 15:13).

Scripture Reading:
Genesis 44:1-18, 30-34

"Will everyone please stand?" Pastor Clark asked. Roger looked up in surprise. He had been so busy drawing funny sketches of different people he hadn't realized the Sunday morning service was almost over.

He glanced at those around him. Most had tears in their eyes. Roger wondered what Pastor Clark had preached to stir them so. He hadn't heard a word. He tuned in.

"I was guilty. I deserved to die," Pastor Clark was saying. "But Jesus took my place at Calvary. He became my substitute."

Quickly, Roger tuned out again. He didn't want to hear about Calvary. For some reason it made him feel guilty.

That afternoon he took his rod and reel and, followed by his little brother, went to the pond.

"I hear dogs coming," Roger warned. "Stay by me, Cliff."

The little boy pointed toward the tree line. "There they are, Roger." Three wild, skinny dogs were glaring at them.

"Ignore them," Roger ordered. "Maybe they'll. . . ."

But he was too late. Cliff had thrown a rock at the dogs. With a deep growl they sprang at the little boy. Cliff screamed as one dog's teeth sank into his leg.

Instantly, Roger jumped into the middle of the pack. With one accord the dogs turned to attack the older boy. As they jumped for Roger's throat, he screamed, "Run, Cliff! Run!"

He felt the bony, wiry body of a dog push against him. A sharp pain ran down his shoulder as he fell to the ground.

When Roger came to, he was in the emergency room. "How. . . ." he started to ask. But the words would not come. There was a tube in his throat and two doctors were leaning over him. Blood was everywhere. Roger groaned. Everything went black again.

When he next opened his eyes, he was in a hospital room. His mother sat by his bed. "Cliff?" he tried to whisper, but the words stuck in the tube.

Mrs. Nelson took his hand. She knew what he was asking. "Cliff's fine, son. Thanks to you. And you're going to be fine, too. Thanks to The Lord. In a day or two they'll take out the tube and you'll be able to talk."

Roger relaxed. When he awoke, the sun was shining and Pastor Clark was standing beside the bed. "You were a very brave young man, Roger, to jump those dogs. You saved Cliff's life. You took his place."

You took his place. The words echoed in Roger's brain. Somewhere he had heard about someone taking someone else's place. Where was it? Then he remembered. Sunday morning. Pastor Clark's altar call: "Jesus took my place at Calvary. He was my substitute."

Suddenly Roger realized what it meant to be a substitute. It was an act of great love. *Why, Jesus loves me as much as I love Cliff,* Roger thought. A warm, happy feeling covered him.

As he drifted off to sleep, he thought, *When they take this tube out, I'm going to tell everybody how much Jesus loves me . . . and how much I love Him.*

The Reason:

(Riddle answer: Benjamin)

To save his father from heartache, Judah offered to take Benjamin's place and stay in Egypt as a slave. Twenty years before he had suggested they sell another brother, Joseph, into slavery. (See Genesis 37:26-27.)

- What do you think changed Judah?
- When Benjamin was arrested, his brothers returned to the city with him. What does this tell you about them?
- Why did Judah offer to take Benjamin's place?
- Why did Jesus become our substitute at Calvary?

What love and grace!
Jesus died in my place.

57

The Finished Product

How was Joseph like a yardstick?

Key Verse:
And we know that all things work together for good to them who love God, to those who are the called according to His purpose (Romans 8:28).

Scripture Reading:
Genesis 45:1-15

The door opened and closed so quietly Mrs. Scott wasn't sure she had heard it. "Jamie? Is that you?" she called.

With slumped shoulders and a long face, Jamie came into the kitchen. "Yeah, it's me," she mumbled.

Mrs. Scott picked up a cup of shortening. "Whatever is the matter, Honey?"

Jamie doubled over the kitchen bar. Her shoulders shook as sobs erupted. "Ooohhh, Mother," she wailed. "Everything's gone wrong. Everything!"

Her mother put an arm around her and waited for the storm to pass. She pulled a paper towel from a roller and handed it to Jamie. "Blow," she ordered. The girl smiled faintly as she obeyed. "Sit down and tell me about it," Mrs. Scott said gently.

Jamie's eyes clouded. "Why does everything bad happen at once?"

Mrs. Scott raked the shortening into a bowl and added sugar. As she stirred, she waited.

Jamie blew her nose again. "My best friend, Lori, is moving. Miss Marshall's putting me in a special reading class. Grandmother has cancer. I've got to wear this dumb headgear to straighten my teeth. How can I make friends when I look like an alien from outer space?"

As Mrs. Scott broke an egg against the edge of the cabinet, she reminded, "You only wear it two hours a day, Honey."

Jamie ignored her. "Why does God let all this happen to me? I thought He loved me." Two tears trickled down her face. "Our Bible verse today said that all things work together for good to those who love God. I love God, but still all these bad things happen to me."

Mrs. Scott scooped a bit of batter onto a spoon. She held it out to Jamie. "Have a bite, honey."

Jamie eyed the spoon suspiciously. "What is it?"

"Shortening, sugar, and egg," Mrs. Scott answered.

"Yuck!" Jamie gagged.

"Then how about a bite of flour or baking soda or cocoa?"

Jamie looked at her mother with a question mark. "No way!"

Mrs. Scott raised her eyebrows. "But, Jamie, you like chocolate cake."

"Sure," Jamie answered. "But not raw eggs or flour or shortening."

Mrs. Scott sifted flour into the mixture. "The Bible says all things work *together* for good. It doesn't say everything is good. Cocoa, flour, baking soda . . . these things alone are not good, but mix them together with sugar and a few other ingredients and. . . ."

"Yummmmmm, good!" Jamie finished.

Mrs. Scott nodded. "Right. Everything that happens to us is not pleasant. But when the bitter is mixed with the sweet, the sad with the happy, the finished product comes out good."

"Like chocolate cake," Jamie grinned.

"Better than chocolate cake," Mrs. Scott responded as she dumped the batter into a pan.

"Don't scrape the bowl, Mother," Jamie said as she pulled a spoon from a cabinet drawer. "I want to."

The Reason:

(Riddle answer: He was a ruler.)

Joseph experienced many bitter things before he understood how things were working together for good in his life.

- Name some of the bitter experiences Joseph had.
- How did these things work together for his good?
- Are some bitter things happening to you? Be patient. God is still adding ingredients. If you will trust Him, the finished product will be good. Yummmmm!

It takes bitter and sweet
To make life complete.

58

God Provides

What was the first vehicle with horsepower?

Key Verse:
And my God shall supply all your need according to His riches in glory by Christ Jesus (Philippians 4:19).

Scripture Reading:
Genesis 45:16-28; 46:26-30

Doug stared at his bowl of oatmeal.

"It's getting cold, Doug," Mrs. Green said as she sat down across from him. "Doug? Douglas Green?"

Doug jerked his head up. "What? Did someone say something to me?"

His parents laughed. "Is your name Douglas Green?"

Doug nodded, unsmiling.

Mr. Green's smile faded. "Is something wrong, son?"

Doug heaved a big sigh. "Last Sunday Mr. Wayne asked me to visit Darrell this week. I promised I would."

"Today is Saturday," Mrs. Green reminded him. Doug groaned, "Yeah, I know. I've got to do it today."

"Don't you want to go see Darrell?" Mr. Green asked.

"Not really," Doug answered honestly. "His dad is dying, and I don't know what to say or do."

"It's not really a matter of doing or saying anything," Mrs. Green replied. "It's more a matter of being there."

Mr. Green pushed his chair back from the table. "I'll make a deal with you, Doug. You help me paint the shutters this morning, and I'll go with you this afternoon."

Doug jumped up. "It's a deal. Let's get started."

Mrs. Green gathered up the breakfast dishes. "Count me in on both projects."

In the garage Doug looked around. "Where's the paint?"

"In the trunk of the car," Mr. Green said. "And the brushes are hanging on the north wall."

The morning passed quickly. "We'll hang the shutters when we get back from the Bakers'," Mr. Green said as he cleaned brushes.

The visit at the Bakers' went so smoothly Doug hated to leave. "I'll be back next week," he promised Darrell.

Darrell beamed. "Great! It sure helps."

As they pulled away from the curb, Doug said, "Thanks, Mom, Dad, for coming with me. I don't know if I could have done it by myself."

Mr. Green caught his eye in the rear-view mirror. "When God gives us a job to do, He always provides the tools."

Doug wrinkled his forehead. "Tools?"

Mr. Green nodded. "This morning when I asked you to help me paint the shutters, did you have to buy the paint and brushes?"

"Of course not," Doug replied. "You did."

"God always gives us the tools, or strength, to do the job He gives us. He supplied the help you needed to visit Darrell by sending your mother and me with you." Mr. Green stopped for a red light.

Darrell spied a familiar arch out the car window. "Say, Dad, I feel kinda weak. How about a Big Mac to strengthen me for the job of hanging shutters?"

Mr. Green chuckled as he flipped on the turn signal. "I know when I've been had. With cheese or without?"

The Reason:

(Riddle answer: wagon. Horses pulled it.)

When Joseph sent his brothers to bring their families and his father to Egypt, he supplied everything they would need for the journey. Likewise, our heavenly Father provides all our needs according to His riches. Never forget, He is very rich indeed.

- Describe in one word how Israel (Jacob) must have felt when he realized his son Joseph was alive.
- Has God ever supplied a need for your family? Tell someone about it today.
- Do you have a special need? Tell God about it now.

Whatever your need today,
God will provide a way.

59

Grandparents Are Grand

What's the nicest thing your grandparents ever gave you?

Key Verse:
One generation shall praise Your works to another (Psalm 145:4).

Scripture Reading:
Genesis 48:1-22

Andy sat drooped on his step stool. "What's the matter, honey?" asked Mrs. Morgan as she knelt beside him.

Two tiny tears crept down the little boy's cheeks. "I was a wishin' I had a grandpa like Steve. He's got two." Andy held up two fingers. "They take him fishin'."

Mrs. Morgan's heart quivered. "I wish you did, too."

"Wish you did what?" asked ten-year-old Sherri as she came into the room.

"Wish I had a grandpa," Andy repeated sadly. "All mine are in heaven with Jesus. I wish I had one here."

Sherri's face brightened. "I've got an idea." She turned to her mother. "You adopted me. Why can't we adopt some grandparents? I'd like to have a grandmother."

"'Dopt a grandma and grandpa?" Andy jumped up and clapped his hands. "Let's do. Let's do. My grandpa can take me fishin' and Sherri's grandma can show her how to . . . how to do somethin'. They can come live with us."

Mrs. Morgan stood up. "Well, I doubt if they'll want to live with us. Do you have anyone in mind, Sherri?"

"How about the Walkers? They live near here and go to our church. . . ."

". . . and they don't have children or grandchildren," Mrs. Morgan put in. "I think they would be perfect."

Andy started for the door. "Let's go right now."

Mrs. Morgan laughed. "Wait. I'd better talk with your dad and then call first."

"And we ought to take them gifts, too. Remember all the things you gave me when you adopted me?" Sherri smiled.

Mrs. Morgan gave her daughter a hug. "I remember. You were a gift from heaven. We wanted to give you everything at once."

As Sherri and Mrs. Morgan arranged a bouquet of flowers to take to the Walkers, Andy made plans. "My grandpa can tell me stories and take me to the zoo and make me a tire swing and. . . ."

"Wait a minute, young man," Mrs. Morgan stopped him. "It won't all be getting. Grandchildren do nice things for their grandparents, too."

Andy puckered his lips. "Well, I guess I could . . . I could take my grandpa fishin' ."

Mrs. Margan and Sherri laughed. Sherri shook a finger at her little brother. "You'd better be good when we go over there; no climbing on the piano or tracking mud on the carpet or they may not adopt you."

Andy looked very serious. "I'll be good. I promise."

The visit to the Walkers was a great success. They were delighted to be adopted and made plans to take Sherri and Andy to the park the next Saturday. As Mrs. Morgan and the children left, Mrs. Walker brushed a tear from her smiling face. "This is the nicest thing that has happened to us in a long time."

Mr. Walker swung Andy up on his shoulders. "How about a ride, Grandson?" he asked.

Andy squealed and clung to Mr. Walker's neck as they jogged out to the car.

Later as they told Mr. Morgan about the new family members, Sherri said, "I know why they call them grandparents. They're grand."

Andy climbed up on his dad's lap. "Know what my grandpa called me? He called me his grandson."

The Reason:

(Riddle answer: your parents)

Imagine what it was like when Joseph's sons met their grandfather for the first time. Israel (Jacob) had never dreamed that he would see his son again, much less see Joseph's sons. What a wonderful surprise blessing!

- Do you have grandparents? If so, thank God for them. Then write them a note telling them how much you love them.
- If you do not have grandparents, why not adopt some? There are many elderly people who are lonely and would love to have some "grand" children.

Grandparents are grand.
Right now give them a hand.

60

The Stress Test

Why is Genesis the first book of the Bible?

Key Verse:
When He has tested me, I shall come forth as gold (Job 23:10).

Scripture Reading:
Genesis 50:15-21

As soon as her grandmother opened the car door, Ashley leaned forward. "What did the doctor say, Gram?"

Grandmother King wrinkled her nose. "He said for me to come back Monday for a stress test."

"A stress test?" echoed Arnold. "That's what we have in school all the time."

Ashley looked at him in disgust. "We don't either."

Arnold laughed, "Yes, we do. Every test I take puts me under stress."

Grandfather started the car. As they drove out of the parking lot, Ashley asked, "What's a stress test, Gram?"

"It's where you do various simple exercises while you are hooked up to a monitor that records your heartbeat. It tells the doctors how much stress your heart can stand," Grandmother explained.

Ashley curled into the corner of the seat. Fear clutched at her heart. She didn't think she could stand it if anything happened to her grandmother. Wasn't it enough that her parents were divorced, and she and Arnold were living with their grandparents?

Sensing Ashley's fears, Grandmother turned with a smile. "Don't worry, honey. God will take care of us."

"Then why. . . ." Ashley began.

Grandfather met her gaze in the rear-view mirror. "We have lots of stress tests in life. The problems that we have show God, and us, what is really in our hearts."

"What do you mean, Gramps?" Ashley asked quietly.

Grandfather continued, "Your parents' divorce has been a stress test for all of us. It has revealed what was really in us."

Ashley bit her fingernail. "At first, I hated them both. But then I realized I really didn't. I guess why it hurt so was because I loved them both so much."

Arnold kicked her shin gently. "Don't bite your fingernail, Ashley."

Quickly, she removed her finger. "I didn't think I'd ever forgive them," she confessed. "But I have."

"Your parents are hurting, too," Grandfather said. "It may be a long time before they learn to forgive each other . . . and themselves."

Arnold fiddled with the armrest. "I'll tell you one good thing that has come out of it."

"What?" Ashley demanded.

"Gram and Gramps take us to church," he smiled widely. "And we've received the Holy Ghost."

The fear clutching Ashley's heart fled. She relaxed. "And maybe soon Mother and Dad will come to church with us."

Grandmother nodded, "That's what we're praying for."

Grandfather smiled over his shoulder. "We may not be making straight A's, kids, but I think we're passing the test."

"And I believe Grandmother will pass her stress test Monday, too," Ashley smiled. "God will take care of us."

The Reason:

(Riddle answer: Because it starts, "In the beginning.")

Joseph's life was a series of stress tests. The final one came when his father died. He could have paid his brothers back for what they did to him, but revenge was not in his heart. Joseph's final report card showed straight As.
- What do you think was Joseph's greatest test?
- What is the hardest trial you have been through?
- Why do you think God allows His children to be tested?
- Who was your favorite character from the Book of Genesis? What did you learn from this person's life?

Do your best.
You'll pass the test.

61

Trapped

What is the strongest trap in the world?

Key Verse:
Therefore if the Son makes you free, you shall be free indeed (John 8:36).

Scripture Reading:
Exodus 1:8-14

"Pop some corn, Kara," Scott called.

"No way," Kara returned from the kitchen. "Who was your servant this time last year?"

Mrs. Baker frowned and shook her head to quieten the shouting match as she said into the telephone, "I know, Margaret. We're praying for him. Keep your chin up." She hung up with a sigh.

"Is Lance gone again?" Kara asked.

Mrs. Baker nodded. "Yes, he's been gone since Saturday."

Kara slammed a cabinet door. "He makes me so mad. He worries Aunt Margaret half to death. I'm ashamed for anyone to know he's my cousin. He's so stupid to run with that gang."

"I feel sorry for him," Mrs. Baker replied.

"Sorry for him?" Kara echoed. "I feel sorry for his mother. If I was Aunt Margaret, I'd. . . ."

From the other room Scott's pleading voice interrupted, "Aren't you going to pop some corn, Kara?"

Kara raised her voice. "I told you, no. I've got more to do than wait on you."

Mrs. Baker ignored the interruption. "Lance is a good kid, but he's bound by drugs. We need to pray for him."

Kara snorted. "I'll save my prayers for Aunt Mar. . . ."

A banging from the garage stopped her.

"What's that?" Scott asked as he came into the kitchen. When he opened the door, they stared in amazement.

"What in the world?" Mrs. Baker exclaimed. A dog's body, with a plastic pitcher for a head, was bumping wildly into everything.

"It's Cuddles," Kara wailed. "She's got her head caught in that pitcher."

"Cuddles, here, girl," Mrs. Baker called to the frightened pup. Kara picked up the dog and cooed gently as Mrs. Baker tried to free her.

"I can't get it off. It's formed a vacuum," she said.

Scott pulled a knife from his pocket. "Hold her still, Kara," he ordered. Carefully, he punctured the pitcher. As air rushed in, the vacuum released, and Mrs. Baker eased the pitcher off the pup's head.

"Oh, thank you, Scott," Kara smiled. As she patted the pup, she crooned. "Poor baby. Your curiosity almost killed you."

Mrs. Baker leaned against the wall. "Apparently, she stuck her nose in the pitcher and then pushed it up against something to hold it as she rammed her head farther inside."

Kara laid the pup against her heart. "Feel my heart pounding, Cuddles? You scared me."

"Cuddles was caught and couldn't help herself," Mrs. Baker remarked, "much as Lance is caught. Curiosity started him using drugs. Now he's in a trap so powerful he cannot break loose. Only God can deliver him. It may be that God wants to use us to help Lance. If so, He will show us how."

Scott nodded, "I'm willing. Lance is a good guy—too good to be trapped." As he opened the door, he winked at Kara, "Now, Sis, will you pop some corn?"

Kara nudged her brother. "Say, please, and I will."

The Reason:

(Riddle answer: sin. Only God can free one from it.)

God's people, the descendants of Jacob (Israel), were trapped in Egypt as slaves to the Egyptians. Sin makes slaves of people, too. When they are trapped by sin, they do things they do not want to do.

- Name some sins that trap people.
- Do you know someone who is caught in one of these traps? Pray for that person right now.
- Has sin trapped you? If so, ask God to set you free. Don't spend another day in sin's trap.

Sin enslaves,
But Jesus saves.

62

A Safe Hiding Place

How was Moses' mother like Noah?

Key Verse:
Hide me under the shadow of Your wings (Psalm 17:8).

Scripture Reading:
Exodus 1:22; 2:1-10

Creak! Creak! Creak! The porch swing sang as Jay pushed with his toes. Mandi and Grandmother sat beside him, rocking back and forth. Grandfather sat on the top porch step, patting Rusty.

"I love to watch the sun go down on the farm. I wish we could stay here forever," Mandi sighed.

Jay shook his head. "You know we can't stay forever. But it would be nice if we could stay longer."

As a flash of lightning crossed the horizon, Mandi shivered, "Is it going to storm, Grandpa?"

Grandfather nodded. "I hope so. We need the rain."

"Oh, I'm scared of storms," Mandi cried.

Cluck! Cluck-cluck-cluck! A flutter of activity across the driveway brought Jay to his feet, stopping the swing.

At the same time Rusty let out a low growl. "Easy there, boy." Grandfather tightened his grip on the dog.

"What's going on?" Jay asked. Grandmother put a finger to her lips. "Sssshhh. Watch."

A mother hen with her wings outstretched was calling urgently, *Cluck-cluckcluckcluck!* From all directions little chicks were scurrying toward her.

"What's wrong with her?" Jay asked. "Is she scared?"

"Look up," Grandmother pointed. A large hawk was circling over the chicken yard. "That hawk is looking for his supper. The mother hen is warning her babies."

Mandi gasped. "Oh, hurry, little chicks, hurry!"

When the last baby was beside her, the mother hen settled her wings down, hiding each one. The hawk circled one more time and disappeared into the darkening clouds.

"Go find your supper somewhere else, old Mr. Hawk," Jay growled as he sat down and started the porch swing again.

"The sky's getting blacker," Mandi worried.

"She's a baby about storms," scoffed Jay.

A streak of lightning ran across the sky, followed by a rumble of thunder. Grandmother stood up. "I'd better close the windows."

Mandi grabbed her grandmother's hand. "I'll go, too."

Grandfather stood up. "We might as well all go in."

He laughed as Rusty headed for the door. "Not you, old boy. Go join your friends in the barn." As they entered the house, the rain started and everything went black.

"Where is everybody?" called a frightened little boy.

"We're right here, Jay," Grandfather put his arm around the boy. "Take about four steps forward. Now sit down on the couch. I'll get a flashlight."

Grandmother and Mandi sat down beside Jay. The wind howled and rain pelted the house.

"Aren't you afraid, Grandmother?" Mandi asked.

"No. I feel like the little chickens."

"Like the chickens?" Jay repeated.

"Yes," Grandmother answered. "I am under the shelter of God's great big wings. It's dark in here, but it's safe."

"God's wings?" Mandi echoed. "Does God have wings?"

Grandmother chuckled, "Not feather wings, but He does put an invisible shelter over His children."

A thin stream of light came down the hall. At that moment light flooded the room. Grandfather laughed, "It never fails. As soon as I get a light, the electricity comes back on."

Grandmother stood up. "Let's close the windows. Then I'll pop some corn. I love to eat popcorn on stormy nights."

Grandfather chuckled, "And every other night, too."

Later as the corn popped in the microwave and the rain plopped on the roof, Mandi curled up at her grandfather's feet. "I'm not scared any more. I like it here under God's wings."

The Reason:

(Riddle answer: She built an ark.)

God took care of baby Moses, and He will take care of you.
- What scares you more than anything else?
- How has God protected you from it in the past?
- Thank God for taking care of you, and ask Him to take away the fear.

It's snug and safe
In God's hiding place.

Right But Wrong

When is right not right?

Key Verse:
All the ways of a man are pure in his own eyes, but the LORD weighs the spirits (Proverbs 16:2).

Scripture Reading:
Exodus 2:11-15

Blaire skipped into the classroom and dropped her books on her desk. "Good morning, Miss Kelly."

"Good morning, Blaire. Where is Steven?"

"This is the day he goes to therapy," Blaire reminded the teacher.

Blaire smiled sweetly at the girl sitting beside her. "Hi, Monica. That sweater looks nice on you. Much nicer than it did on me. I never really liked it."

A crushed look crossed Monica's face, but Blaire didn't notice.

At lunch she was sitting with Amy, when Amy muttered, "Guess who's going to sit across from us?"

Blaire looked up and groaned. "Oh, no! Alicia."

Amy whispered behind her hand, "Just because this is a Christian school doesn't mean everyone is a Christian! Her folks just sent her here to keep her out of trouble."

"I can believe that!" Blaire answered.

"Believe what?" Alicia asked as she sat down.

"Nothing of interest to you," Blaire responded.

"Yeah? You mean nothing you want me to know," Alicia countered. "Say, where's your bird-brained brother?"

Like a flash, Blaire's hand shot out. The slap rang through the lunchroom. There was a moment's stunned silence. Then Alicia jumped to her feet. "Miss Kelly, Blaire slapped me!"

Blaire's eyes shot sparks of fire. "I'll do it again, too, if you ever. . . ."

Miss Kelly put a hand on each girl's arm. "Come with me." After she had sorted out the facts, Miss Kelly said, "You may go, Alicia. I'll talk to you after school."

When the other girl was gone, Blaire sobbed, "I didn't think anyone here would laugh at Steven because he's intellectually disabled. They did that at public school, but this is a Christian school. At least, it's supposed to be."

Miss Kelly nodded. "Yes, it's supposed to be. But the school is no better than the students who attend it. You, Blaire, had a right to be angry when Alicia made fun of Steven, but you had no right to slap her. It is possible to be right but wrong."

Blaire looked puzzled. Miss Kelly continued, "It is right to defend your brother, but the way you did it was wrong. It is also possible to do the right thing for the wrong reason."

"How?" Blaire asked.

Miss Kelly said softly, "For example, by giving your hand-me-down clothes to someone and then making them feel like beggars."

Blaire's face flushed. "But, Miss Kelly, I didn't . . . I mean, I didn't intend to put Monica down."

"I know you didn't intend to, but you did," Miss Kelly replied. "That's doing the right thing for the wrong reason. Your motive was to make yourself look better than Monica."

Blaire looked at the floor. "I'm sorry, Miss Kelly."

Miss Kelly stood up. "Since this is your first offense, you get off with a reprimand. Just don't let this happen again. Remember it's possible to be right but wrong."

Blaire nodded. "Right! I'll remember."

The Reason:

(Riddle answer: when right is left)

God places emphasis both on what we do and why we do it. He weighs our spirit (attitude). For the results to be right, both the motive (reason) and the action must be right.
- How was Moses right but wrong in defending his Hebrew brethren? What was the results?
- Can you think of some ways in which we can be right but wrong? How about witnessing?

Not just what, but why,
Determines your reward by and by.

64

Pay Attention

What animal runs a mint?

Key Verse:
Give ear, O my people, to my law: incline your ears to the words of my mouth (Psalm 78:1).

Scripture Reading:
Exodus 3:1-10

It had been a terrible week for Greg. He had made an F in math. "But, Miss Mason," he had argued. "I didn't know you gave us an assignment."

"That's because you weren't paying attention," his teacher had replied.

He had also been left home when his parents had gone shopping because he hadn't been ready. "Why didn't you tell me to get ready?" he had asked.

His mother had sighed. "I did . . . three times, but you weren't listening."

And to cap it all off, on Sunday morning, he discovered that he had missed a fishing trip because he hadn't bothered to read the note his Sunday school teacher had given him.

All the way home from church his mind was filled with grumbling questions: *Why am I always the one left out? Why am I always in trouble? Why is everyone picking on me?*

He was so engrossed in his thoughts that he didn't hear his mother say, "Greg, I want you to clean your room this afternoon."

After dinner four-year-old Nanci followed him into his room. "Show me how to tie my shoe," she begged.

Grumbling, Greg sat the little girl on the edge of his unmade bed. "First, you take this string and hold it in this hand." He placed a shoelace in Nanci's hand. "And then you. . . ."

"What's that poster say?" asked Nanci, pointing at the wall.

Greg frowned. "Nanci, pay attention."

The little girl wiggled. "I wish I could read."

"Do you want to learn to tie your shoes or not?"

"Sure," Nanci answered. "Show me."

Greg took a deep breath. "Put this other lace in your other hand." Nanci grabbed the lace. "Now cross this one over like this," He guided her hands.

She looked around. "Boy, Greg, your room is messy."

"Are you going to pay attention or not?" Greg snapped.

Nanci jumped down. "I will tomorrow. My mind's too busy to sit still."

Greg shook his head as the little girl ran from the room. "Oh, brother! Or should I say, 'Oh, sister'?" He picked up his ball glove and started down the hall. Then he stopped and stared in amazement. Blocking the hall was a chair holding a big sign: "Stop! Do not pass this point until your room is clean!"

"Mom!" Greg yelled. "What's this sign for?"

"For you," returned Mrs. Davidson from the kitchen. "I had to do something to get your attention."

At that moment there was a crash in the living room. Nanci's wail filled the house. Mrs. Davidson went running. Greg stood behind the hall barrier and listened. "What happened, Nanci?" Mrs. Davidson asked.

"I fell," the little girl sobbed. "I t-t-tripped on my s-s-shoe string. Greg didn't tie it for me."

Greg's mouth fell open. *I didn't tie it? She didn't tie it! She wouldn't pay attention long enough to learn how. No wonder she fell . . . no wonder . . .* His thoughts slowed. *No wonder I failed my math test, and got left home, and missed the fishing trip . . . no wonder.*

He turned and went back down the hall to his room. Aloud he said, "I, Greg Davidson, do hereby pledge from this day forward to pay attention."

The Reason:

(Riddle answer: the skunk—He makes scents.)

God has a special message for each one of us. To find out what it is, we must pay attention to His Word. If we do not listen, God may have to use drastic measures to get our attention.

- How did God get Moses' attention? How did Mrs. Davidson get Greg's attention?
- What was the message God gave Moses? What was the message Greg's mother had for him?
- Why is it important that you pay attention to your parents? to the preaching of God's Word?

Got troubles? For prevention,
Remember—pay attention.

65

Excuses, Excuses

What is most kids' favorite excuse?

Key Verse:
But the LORD said to me: "Do not say, I am a youth," for you shall go to all to whom I send you, and whatever I command you, you shall speak (Jeremiah 1:7).

Scripture Reading:
Exodus 4:10-17

"We need volunteers to pass out revival handbills Saturday afternoon," Mr. James told his preteen boys. Eyeballs rolled. Arms paralyzed. Groans rumbled. Mr. James raised his eyebrows. "No volunteers? Then I guess I'll have to do you like God did Moses—draft you."

"Ahhhh, Brother James," moaned Taylor. "Have a heart."

"I'm busy Saturday," Jason said. "I've got to . . . ahhhh . . . got to . . . ahhhh do something."

Mr. James grinned as the boys laughed. "And that something is pass out handbills." Mr. James winked at Jason.

"I've got a corn on my toe," Nelson invented.

"And I've got to pick corn," Taylor told them.

"Pick corn in April?" Mr. James asked.

Taylor grimaced, "Plant corn? It's something corny."

"And I've got to sell popcorn for the craft sale," Pete said. Under his breath, he muttered, "Saturday morning."

"I've got the corniest class in this church," Mr. James chuckled. "Nevertheless, we will pass out the revival handbills for Pastor Wise. I promised. Meet me here at 2:00 Saturday afternoon. There'll be pizza later."

"Pizza?" the boys echoed. "Oh, well. . . ."

"In that case," Taylor said, "the corn can wait."

Saturday afternoon the boys met at the church. "Can we just put the handbill on the door and run?" Taylor asked.

Mr. James shook his head. "No. Ring the doorbell and give everyone a personal invitation. If they aren't home, slip it inside the storm door. But do not put it in the mailbox. That's against the law!"

Taylor moaned, "I don't know what to say. The minute the door opens, I'll get tongue-tied; I know I will."

"You sound like Moses," Mr. James grinned. "You can go in pairs, like Moses and Aaron."

After the teams were chosen, the boys prayed, and then loaded in Mr. James's minivan. "We'll start on First Street. Taylor and Jason, you get out here. Go around this block."

As they watched the van disappear, Taylor took a deep breath. "Come on, Aaron, let's get started."

"Aaron?" Jason repeated. "Why are you calling me Aaron?"

Taylor grinned, "Cause you're going to do the talking, buddy, that's why!"

The boys were surprised to find that Mr. Mason, their science teacher, lived at the second house. When Jason invited him, Mr. Mason smiled, "My wife was saying yesterday that we needed to go to church. My grandmother was Pentecostal. When does this revival start?"

"Tomorrow night," Taylor said. "At 6:30. You'll like our church, Mr. Mason. It's exciting."

Mr. Mason nodded. "That's what I remember about my grandmother's church. Look for us, boys. We'll be there."

"Great!" Taylor beamed. "See you tomorrow night."

As the boys went out the gate, Jason said, "Just two houses, and already someone has promised to come."

Taylor quickened his step. "Hurry up, Moses."

"Moses?" Jason barked. "I thought I was Aaron."

Taylor grinned. "You can't do all the talking. It's my turn now."

The Reason:
(Riddle answer: "I forgot.")

When God chooses someone to do a job, He's smart enough to pick the right person. When we argue with God's choice, we are saying, "God, I'm smarter than You." And that's a dumb thing to say!
- Why do you think Moses was afraid to do what God asked him to do?
- What excuse did Moses make? Why didn't God accept Moses' excuse?
- Have you ever made an excuse for not obeying God's Word? What happened?

Don't try to shirk;
Excuses don't work.

66

Double Trouble

Who was the first person to blame someone else for his trouble?

Key Verse:
Many are the afflictions of the righteous, but the LORD delivers him out of them all (Psalm 34:19).

Scripture Reading:
Exodus 5:1-9, 22-23

The Martins sped down the freeway through the night. Melissa asked from the back seat. "How much farther?"

Mr. Martin glanced at the odometer. "Seventy-five miles."

"Is Grandpa going to die?" Melissa whispered.

"We pray not," Mrs. Martin answered quietly. The lights of an oncoming car revealed the worry lines on her face.

"What's going to happen next?" Melissa asked.

"I don't know," Mr. Martin replied as he dimmed the light. "It hasn't been a very good year, has it?"

"Maybe something good will happen," Mrs. Martin suggested.

Melissa leaned back. "It's about time something good happened to us. First, Daddy lost his job and was out of work for three months, then I broke my arm, then Andy had hepatitis, and now Grandpa's had a heart attack."

"We know all that, honey," Mrs. Martin said. "There's no need to recount our troubles. We should be counting our blessings."

"It was just a year ago this month that we found the truth," Mr. Martin reminded them. "The Lord has filled us with the Holy Ghost, and we have a lovely church family!"

"But," Melissa argued, "it seems like we've had double trouble since we got in church. I thought things would get better, not worse."

"Many things are better," Mrs. Martin said. "Our marriage is much better; our family closer, and my nerves calmer."

As the car lights fell on a road sign, Mr. Martin exclaimed, "Cedarvale? Look at the map, Linda."

Mrs. Martin flipped open her phone. She moaned, "We should have turned off the interstate fifteen miles back."

Mr. Martin patted his wife's hand. "Sorry about that, honey. I know you're anxious to get to your dad."

Mrs. Martin smiled sadly, "It can't be helped."

Melissa remembered a time when such a mistake would have sent her mother into a screaming fit. There was no doubt about it: God had done a lot for her family. But why so much trouble?

Fifteen miles back down the road, Mr. Martin turned onto a narrow, two-lane highway. He flipped off the cruise control and slowed their speed. "Won't make very good time on this highway, I'm afraid," he apologized.

"No," Mrs. Martin replied, "but we are headed in the right direction. We were making good time on the interstate, but we would never have reached the hospital."

Mr. Martin nodded. "Before we got in church, life seemed smoother, but we were headed the wrong direction."

Melissa snapped to attention. "So that's it. We've had double trouble this last year, but at least, we're on the right road—the road to Heaven."

"Look ahead," Mr. Martin exclaimed. "A new four-lane road. Looks like things are going to get better."

"And so is Grandpa," Mrs. Martin declared. "I feel like God just assured me of that. And know what else I believe?"

"What?" Melissa asked.

"The roughest part of our journey is over. From this night on, things are going to get better for the Martins. It's like Dad always says, 'Nothing last forever—not even trouble.'"

Melissa smiled as she curled up in the corner to sleep.

The Reason:

(Riddle answer: Adam, when he blamed Eve. See Genesis 3:12.)

Just when the Israelites expected freedom, POW!, the chains of slavery tightened. But finally, they were on the right road, headed toward deliverance.
- Why did the people blame Moses for their trouble?
- What would you say to encourage someone in the church who is having double trouble?

This one thing I know,
Troubles come; troubles go.

67

Which Is Greater?

Who owned the first hot rod?

Key Verse:
He who is in you is greater than he who is in the world (I John 4:4).

Scripture Reading:
Exodus 7:7-13

Carson curled his fingers. "These demons have long, grasping arms with claws like an eagle." He raised his voice so he could be heard above the school-bus clatter. "They swoop down out of black clouds and latch onto people. When they do, the people go crazy. They get guns and start shooting people down. Bang! Bang! Bang!" He pointed a finger at Jordan.

Jordan shivered. Carson continued, "It's the spookiest movie I ever saw. Too bad you don't have a TV, Jordan. Think of all the good things you miss."

"Yeah," Rich added, "you didn't even see the movie about the teenage Ninja turtles that crawled out of the sewer. Man, they had power like you wouldn't believe . . . turtle power!"

The boys gathered their books as the bus staggered to a stop. Another school day had begun.

Apparently, every kid in Jordan's class had seen the demon movie but him; even Mr. Wheeler, the teacher, had watched it. Everyone seemed possessed by it.

When Jordan got off the bus that afternoon, he hurried toward home. He wanted to shut out talk of demons and snipers.

Suddenly, a big, wild-looking dog appeared out of nowhere. He lunged at Jordan. Jordan screamed and ran.

"Stand still, Jordan!" ordered a man's voice. Jordan froze. Over his shoulder, he saw Mr. Newman, the postman, pointing a spray can at the dog that had turned on him. *Psssst!* A fine mist hit the dog. Instantly, the dog buried his face in the grass, whining and twisting.

"Get in the house, son," Mr. Newman ordered, "before he realizes what hit him. He's not hurt, just stunned."

Jordan ran for home as Mr. Newman jumped in his cart and drove off. *What a wild day,* Jordan thought, as he collapsed on the sofa. *Demons and dogs. Whew!*

Sometime after midnight, he bolted up in bed, eyes wide, peering into the darkness. "Mamma! Daddy!" he screamed. A shiver ran through him as the darkness closed in on him.

Click! He blinked as light flooded the room. "What's the matter, Jordan?" Mrs. Knight asked as she hugged him.

As his trembling calmed, the boy whispered, "Demons . . . there were demons in here."

Mr. Knight sat down on the bed. "If so, they were just in your head. Your mind has been filled with fear today."

Mrs. Knight said softly, "We don't have to fear demons, Jordan. We have the Holy Ghost. And 'He who is in you is greater than he who is in the world,'" she quoted.

"But," Jordan argued, "it seemed so real. They had evil eyes and horrible bodies. They jumped at me like that dog!"

"What happened when that dog jumped at you today?" Mr. Knight asked.

"Mr. Newman sprayed him with something and stopped him in his tracks," Jordan remembered.

Mr. Knight nodded, "That's what we can do to demons; stop them in their tracks. When they try to attack us, all we have to do is call the name of Jesus in faith. They cannot withstand Jesus' name. Let's pray."

After they had prayed, Mrs. Knight tucked the cover around Jordan. "If you have another bad dream," she said, "just say, 'Jesus.'"

"I will," Jordan yawned. "But I don't think those demons will be back. They wouldn't dare." And he was asleep before his parents reached their room.

The Reason:
(Riddle answer: Moses and Aaron)

It would be foolish to say there are no demons, because there are. Neither can we say that they have no power, because they do. But the Holy Ghost is greater than all the demons put together. When we have the Spirit of God in us, we have nothing to fear.
- What caused Jordan to be afraid?
- Why is it important that we talk and think about good things?
- How do you know that Pharaoh's magicians had power? How do you know that Moses and Aaron had more power?

To keep evil spirits away,
Call on Jesus every day.

68

Hard-Headed Howard

Say this tongue twister five times in a row.
Hard heads, hard hearts.

Key Verse:
For He put on righteousness as a breastplate, and a helmet of salvation on His head (Isaiah 59:17).

Scripture Reading:
Exodus 7:14-25

Howard stood, clutching the back of the pew. *Will church ever be over?* he wondered as Pastor Garrison gave the altar call. It was past noon already.

He could feel his mother willing him to go to the altar. But he wasn't ready to take that step—although every time the invitation was made, his heart did strange things.

I'm just a kid, he reassured himself. *Just twelve years old—today!* And with that thought, he busied his mind with planning the party he was having that afternoon.

Finally, church was over, and Howard gathered his three best friends: Mike, Joe, and Craig. His parents were taking them out to eat at the place of Howard's choosing. Then they had the whole afternoon to celebrate!

When they arrived home, Mr. Drake opened the garage door. "Wow!" four boys whooped. A brand-new ten-speed bike sat in the center of the garage. The boys tumbled from the car.

"It's the very one I wanted," Howard said as he straddled it. "It's supposed to go thirty to forty miles an hour."

Mr. Drake laughed, "I imagine it will if you have the wind and leg power."

"Better open the package beside it," Mrs. Drake said.

For the first time Howard noticed the square box. He ripped into it. "A helmet!" he exclaimed. "Why a helmet?"

"This is a racing bike, son," Mrs. Drake said. "You need to wear a helmet when you ride it."

"Ahhhh Mom" Howard argued "You've always said that I have a hard head. I don't need a helmet."

"I don't deny you have a hard head," Mrs. Drake smiled. "But it's not as hard as the pavement."

While Mr. and Mrs. Drake took their Sunday afternoon naps, the boys took turns riding the new bike, wearing the helmet . . . until it was Howard's second turn.

"I'm not going to wear that hot old helmet," he declared, as he jumped on the bike and flew down the drive.

He was halfway down the block when a cat ran in front of him. He swerved, missed the cat, and hit the curb. The bike flipped. Howard went sailing through the air. He landed in the middle of the street on his knees and elbows. Blood and tears flew.

Craig went to get Mr. and Mrs. Drake, while Mike and Joe ran to help Howard. He was sitting on the curb, crying as much for his bike as himself, when his parents came running.

After reassuring themselves that nothing was broken on Howard or the bike, Mrs. Drake asked, "Where's your helmet?"

Howard hung his head. "In the garage." He looked up. "A helmet wouldn't have helped my knees and elbows. I didn't hurt my head."

"Thank the Lord," said Mr. Drake. "Had it been your head it could have been very serious. And next time it might be."

"Next time I'll be wearing my helmet," Howard promised as he staggered to his feet.

That evening at church Howard stood between the pews as the invitation was given. His elbows throbbed. His knees ached. His heart was pounding. *I guess I've been hardheaded long enough,* he thought. *I don't want to become hardhearted, too.*

With that decision, he limped to the altar and knelt on two very tender knees, while God made one hard-headed boy into a soft-hearted young man.

The Reason:

Pharaoh was hard-headed (stubborn) and hard-hearted (uncaring). Because he was, the Egyptians suffered many things.

- Why is it bad to be hard-headed? hard-hearted?
- How can one person's hard-headedness or hard-heartedness cause others to suffer?
- Have you ever suffered because someone was stubborn or uncaring? Have you ever caused someone to suffer?

A hard head makes a hard heart.
You'll live for God if you're smart.

69

One More Night

What is always coming, but never arrives?

Key Verse:
Behold, now is the accepted time; behold, now is the day of salvation (II Corinthians 6:2).

Scripture Reading:
Exodus 8:1-15

Eeeeek!" Jodi screeched as she flipped on the light. Hundreds (or was it thousands?) of cockroaches went scurrying across the kitchen floor.

Mrs. Parks came running. "What's the. . . . ? Oh, no! The landlord promised to have this apartment sprayed before we moved in. I'll call him first thing in the morning. Go back to bed, honey. There's nothing we can do tonight."

Jodi got a drink and then tiptoed down the hall behind her mother. The thought of squashing a cockroach between her toes almost sent her into spasms.

An hour later, she was still tossing and turning. When she closed her eyes, she saw cockroaches. But when she opened them, she thought. And she didn't want to think.

Ever since Angela had moved to Centerville and started going to their church, Jodi had been filled with jealousy and bitterness. Angela had everything—everything that Jodi didn't have—a nice home, a dad, pretty clothes, the Holy Ghost. . . .

At this point, Jodi tried to turn her thoughts off. She didn't want to think about the Holy Ghost. It made her feel so empty and lonely, even frightened. She wanted the Holy Ghost. She really did. Every night she promised herself, "Tomorrow I'll pray." But she never did.

Finally, she drifted into a troubled sleep and dreamed about giant cockroaches that wore pretty clothes. The next afternoon Jodi asked, "Mother, what did the landlord say about the cockroaches?"

"He promised to send the exterminator over tomorrow."

Jodi shivered. "Tomorrow? Why not today?"

"I guess they're busy," her mother replied. "We'll just have to make the best of it for one more night."

But the exterminator did not come the next day or the next—or the next.

"Mother," Jodi asked one morning, "when is the landlord going to do something about these cockroaches?"

"Tomorrow," Mrs. Parks replied.

"Tomorrow?" Jodi wailed. "That's what he said yesterday. Why do we have to live with cockroaches another day? Why don't they spray today?"

Jodi stared into space as her brain whirled, *Tomorrow? That's what you said yesterday. Why do you live with a guilty conscience another day? Why don't you pray today?*

"What's the matter, Jodi?" Mrs. Parks asked.

Jodi shook her head to clear her brain. "Nothing . . . I . . . I mean, I was just thinking." Tears welled in her eyes. "Mother, would you pray with me right now? I'm so tired of feeling guilty and sinful. I can't stand to feel this way another day."

Mrs. Parks smiled through her tears as she knelt beside her daughter. And what a prayer meeting they had! Soon Jodi's face was glowing, and she was speaking in tongues.

When they had finished praying, Jodi stood. "I've got to call Angela and tell her I just received the Holy Ghost!"

As she started for the telephone, it rang. She picked up the receiver. "Hello . . . Yes, this is the Parks' residence . . . What? You'll be over when? . . . Sure, that's great!"

When she hung up, she turned to her mother with a big smile. "Guess what. The exterminator is coming over right now! We won't have to spend another night with cockroaches or a guilty conscience. Will I ever sleep tonight!"

The Reason:

(Riddle answer: tomorrow)

What a foolish, proud man Pharaoh was. When Moses asked, "When do you want me to get rid of the frogs?" Pharaoh answered, "Tomorrow."

- Why do you think Pharaoh didn't say, "Right now"?
- Do you need to get rid of a guilty conscience? How long have you been saying, "Tomorrow I will"? Do it right now. Don't spend another night with the frogs!

Tomorrow is a lifetime away;
Whatever you need to do, do it today.

70

A World of Difference

How much difference is there between the world and the church?

Key Verse:
I will make a difference between My people and your people (Exodus 8:23).

Scripture Reading:
Exodus 8:16-24

"Aunt Rhoda lets Ranae do whatever she wants. She doesn't order her around like a servant," Melanie raged. "Why can't you be like her?"

As her mother left the room, Melanie was sorry, but she didn't say so. *If only my folks weren't so strict,* she thought.

The next morning Mr. Wills announced, "I have to attend a convention in Chicago next week, Wanda. Why don't you go? Melanie could stay with Ranae."

"Ranae?" Melanie repeated. "But . . ."

"But what?" Mrs. Wills asked.

"Well, it's kinda . . . ahhh dirty over there."

Mrs. Wills shrugged. "But think of all the freedom you will have." So, even though Melanie wasn't excited about it, it was arranged for her to stay with Ranae.

When Melanie brought in her suitcase, Aunt Rhoda took her eyes off the TV long enough to giggle. "You girls will have a blast!" The air was heavy with cigarette smoke.

"Just dump your suitcase on the bed," Ranae invited.

Melanie blinked. *And Mother thinks my room is messy!*

"What do you want to do tonight?" Ranae asked.

Melanie pointed at her notebook. "I've got homework."

"But you're on vacation," Ranae argued. "Let's watch a video. I've got one that'll really educate you!"

A warning bell went off in Melanie's head. "My mom's pretty particular about the videos I watch."

"Yeah, but you're at my house now. My mom doesn't care what I watch if it doesn't interfere with her programs."

"Anybody home?" called a gruff voice from the front hall.

"Dad's home. Let's go see what goodies he's brought."

Melanie followed Ranae into the kitchen where she unloaded a sack. "Pepperoni pizza, cookies, chips." Ranae giggled as she pulled out a six-pack of beer. "Guess we'll leave this for you, Dad."

Uncle Bob grinned, "Good idea. What have you girls got planned for tonight? We want to show Melanie a good. . . ." His words were lost in a spasm of coughing.

"Been smoking too much," scolded Aunt Rhoda as she waddled into the kitchen.

Uncle Bob gasped, "Look w-w-who's talkin." You'll die of lung cancer before I do, if you don't die of malnutrition first."

"I could lose some weight if you didn't bring home fattening foods every night," Aunt Rhoda snapped.

"And I wouldn't have to bring them home if you'd turn off the TV and cook for your family," Uncle Bob returned.

Melanie was embarrassed. Her parents never talked like that!

The week dragged. There were no rules, no chores, no orders. In all her life, Melanie had never heard so much fussing, breathed so much smoke, and eaten so much pizza.

The night before Melanie was to leave, Ranae turned over in bed and whispered, "I bet you'll be glad to go home and get out of this mess," Ranae choked. "I think my folks are going to get a divorce. I wish they were like your mom and dad. I wish they'd go to church. Your home is different—quiet and peaceful and clean and happy and ordered."

Ordered? Melanie thought. *A week ago I didn't want order or to be ordered; I wanted freedom. How dumb I was.*

The Reason:

(Riddle answer: a world of difference)

God drew a line between His people and the Egyptians. There is still a difference between God's people and the rest of the world.

- How did God show a difference between the Israelites and Egyptians?
- Name some differences in Ranae's home and Melanie's.
- Do you live in a Christian home? If so, thank God for your home right now. Then write your parents a thank-you note.

Between the world and the church is a line,
For God says, "I take care of Mine."

71

Sin's Chains

What did the sixth plague do to Pharaoh?

Key Verse:
Do you not know that to whom you present yourselves slaves to obey, you are that one's slaves? (Romans 6:16).

Scripture Reading:
Exodus 9:1-12

Brad gasped and choked. Quickly, he turned so the other guys couldn't see his face. He knew they would laugh.

"How do you like it?" Billy asked.

Brad caught his breath and then croaked. "It's great!"

Great? his conscience jeered. *Now you've not only smoked, you've lied.*

"Sometimes it's a little strong the first time," Eddie sympathized. "But you'll get used to it."

Get used to it? his conscience echoed. *Now they'll expect you to smoke with them all the time.*

"Say, look at the time!" Billy exclaimed. "I've gotta beat it 'fore I get a beatin'. See you tomorrow, same time, same place. Your turn to bring the smokes, Eddie," he called as he ran down the alley.

Eddie shrugged, "Yeah, if I can. My dad's getting suspicious." He hopped on his bike. "Why don't you bring 'em, Brad? No one would ever suspect *you* of stealing cigarettes," he sneered.

So now you're gonna steal, too? Brad's conscience jabbed him.

Brad broke into a sweat and a run. *Hush!* he silently ordered his conscience. *Leave me alone!*

He was several blocks from home when a car pulled up beside him. A familiar voice asked, "Want a ride, son?" Brad's heart flipped. "I . . . uhhhhh . . . yeah, I guess so." He climbed in beside his dad.

"Have a good day?" Mr. Myers edged the car back into the traffic.

"Yeah, pretty good," Brad mumbled.

Mr. Myers frowned, then sniffed. "What do I smell? It smells like cigarette smoke." He glanced at Brad's red face. "It's pretty hard to cover up the smell of tobacco, especially around someone who doesn't smoke. Better tell me about it, son."

Brad's face crumbled. "I didn't want to do it. I don't know why I did." Then he told his dad how he had allowed Eddie and Billy to bully him.

When they stopped at a traffic light, Mr. Myers said, "There is a story about a man who forged chains. He bragged that he could break any chain except one forged by himself. By and by he angered the king for some reason and was thrown in prison. But he wasn't worried. He thought he would simply break the chain. Then he looked at the chain that bound him. It had his trademark on it."

Brad gulped. "Are you saying that the strongest chains are the ones we forge ourselves?"

Mr. Myers nodded. "Right. You are a child of God, Brad, and no one can force you to sin. Not even Satan. God has given you the right to choose what you do. If you become chained by tobacco or any other sinful habit, it will be because you choose to. No one is to blame but yourself. And you are the one who will suffer."

Brad hid his face in his hands. "I know. Look at Uncle Cecil. He's a slave to cigarettes."

Mr. Myers turned the car into the driveway. "Yes, and they're killing him."

Brad reached for the door handle. "I'm sorry, Dad. I won't do it again. I promise." He jumped out of the car. "No chains for me! I like my freedom."

The Reason:
(Riddle answer: made him "boil"ing mad)

It's not always easy to get free from sin's chains. It's best never to allow Satan to put his handcuffs on you.
- Name the six plagues you have read about so far.
- Why was Pharaoh so determined not to let the Israelites go? Why does Satan fight to keep us in bondage?
- Pray right now for someone who is a slave to sin to be delivered. If sin has bound you, ask God to set you free.

That first cigarette is a bad mistake;
It forges a chain that is hard to break.

72

Warning!

Brain twister: How could this be true? Jesus will come at morning, noon, and night.

Key Verse:
Therefore we must give the more earnest heed to the things which we have heard (Hebrews 2:1).

Scripture Reading:
Exodus 9:13-26

Dark, threatening clouds tumbled overhead as the Wells family drove home from church. "Jesus is coming in the clouds," four-year-old Austin said as he intently watched the sky. "Do you think He's coming today?"

"He could," Mrs. Wells replied.

"I've heard that all my life!" scoffed thirteen-year-old Kim. "I think preachers just say that to scare people into being good."

"Why, Kim!" Mrs. Wells was shocked. "Surely you. . . ."

Her words were drowned out by the thin, piercing wail of the storm siren. The wind began to blow fiercely. Large drops of rain pelted the car.

"Oh, a tornado!" Kim cried above the noise. "Hurry, Daddy! Let's get to the cellar."

"Keep calm," Mr. Wells answered, peering through the blinding rain. "We're almost home."

"Maybe Jesus is coming," Austin said excitedly.

"Don't say that!" Kim wailed. "I don't have the Holy Ghost. Hurry, Daddy!"

"Calm down, Kim," Mr. Wells repeated as he turned the car into the driveway. Hail began to salt the ground as the car rolled into the garage. They jumped out and ran for the cellar.

Next door Mr. Stacy stood on his porch, watching the clouds. "Better come to the cellar with us," Mr. Wells called as they ran passed him.

Mr. Stacy laughed, "No, thanks. They blow that siren every time a little cloud comes up. They can't scare me. No need to hide in a dark hole in the ground."

As the cellar door closed behind them, a loud roar filled the air.

"Is it Jesus coming?" Austin asked.

"I told you to stop talking about that!" Kim ordered; "I don't want to hear it."

Mr. Wells lit the oil lamp as Mrs. Wells brushed the dust off the folding chairs. "Whether you want to hear it or not doesn't change the facts, Kim. Jesus is coming," Mrs. Wells said as she sat down.

The sound of hail hitting the vent pipes drowned out further conversation. Austin's eyes sparkled with excitement. But Kim huddled in her chair, trembling.

About half an hour later, the rain slacked, and Mr. Wells left the cellar to see what had happened. When he returned, his face was grim. "It was a tornado. It took part of the roof off our house. Mr. Stacy's house is demolished."

"What about Mr. Stacy?" Kim asked.

"He's on his way to the hospital. Too bad he didn't heed the warning," Mr. Wells said sadly.

Mrs. Wells looked at her frightened daughter. "Kim, don't be foolish like Mr. Stacy. Do you see now why preachers are sounding the warning? Jesus might not come today—but again He might. And you need to get ready."

Kim nodded, "I know, and I'm going to—today."

"Boy," exclaimed Austin as he stuck his head out the cellar door and saw the damage, "I'm sure glad they blew that old siren. When I grow up, I think I'll be a siren blower."

The Reason:

(Riddle answer: When it is day on one side of the earth, it is night on the other.)

God has always given warning when judgment was coming so people could prepare.
- What happened to the Egyptians who heeded Moses' warning of hail? What happened to those who did not believe?
- When was the last time you heard a preacher sound the warning that Jesus is coming soon?
- Are you ready for Christ's return? Have you obeyed Acts 2:38?

Don't be foolish. Heed the warning.
Jesus could come night, noon, or morning.

73

Bugs in the Works

Why did Pharaoh hate Moses?

Key Verse:
Create in me a clean heart, O God, and renew a steadfast spirit within me (Psalm 51:10).

Scripture Reading:
Exodus 10:12-23

Uncle Wayne stuck his head in the door of Bruce's bedroom. "Want to go to the office with me?"

Bruce jumped out of bed. "I sure do!" He loved to goof around in Uncle Wayne's office and pretend he was a big shot. He reached for his shirt, then stopped. "But Mom probably won't let me. I've been grounded!"

Uncle Wayne winked. "I know, but she's making an exception—this time."

Bruce slung on his shirt.

"Better check those buttons," Uncle Wayne laughed. "You either have one button too many or you're one buttonhole short."

Later, as they sped down the freeway toward Uncle Wayne's office in a downtown high-rise building, Bruce asked, "Why are you working on Saturday morning?"

"The computer system has some bugs in it."

"Really? What kind of bugs? Are you going to spray?"

Uncle Wayne laughed, "I don't mean bug bugs; I mean bug problems."

Bruce grinned, "Oh, I know about them. My folks bug me all the time." He grew serious. "'Clean up your room.' 'Take out the trash.' 'Do your homework.'"

Uncle Wayne raised his eyebrows. "Oh?"

"And they're always on me about my attitude." Bruce was getting wound up, now that he had an audience. "They're onto my case about church now. 'Don't sit in the back,' 'Why didn't you go to the altar?' 'Learn your memory verse.' I can't even chew gum without someone buggin' me."

"My, my!" Uncle Wayne teased as he pulled into the parking garage. "You do have a hard life."

Bruce scowled. "I thought you would understand."

As Uncle Wayne squeezed the car into a parking space, he nodded, "Oh, I do. I do."

Later, Bruce sat in a leather chair and propped his feet up on a large desk while his uncle worked on the computer. "When this thing is broken down," he told his nephew, "it just about shuts down the whole business from coast to coast. One bug or simple little mistake can make the whole thing go kablooie."

"How do you find the bug?"

"It's not always easy," Uncle Wayne replied. "But that's my job."

A couple of hours later, he stood and stretched his cramped limbs. "That's it. It's fixed," he announced.

As they drove home, Uncle Wayne sighed, "I'd planned to go fishing today."

"That bug sure messed up your day," Bruce sympathized.

Uncle Wayne nodded. "Bugs have a way of doing that. Attitude bugs can cause lots of problems, too."

Bruce looked out the side window. "Has my mom been talking to you?"

"Yes, sir," Uncle Wayne answered. "And I'm concerned. Seems you've been pretty nasty lately."

"But they bug me. . . ." Bruce began.

"They're just trying to debug you," Uncle Wayne said. "You've pretty well clogged up the works."

"Well, I guess I haven't been an angel," Bruce admitted. He chuckled, "I thought they were bugging me, but I guess it's been the other way around. I'll work on it."

Uncle Wayne squeezed Bruce's shoulder. "Thanks, pal. Now I see some golden arches ahead, and my stomach's buggin' me. I could use a hamburger. How about you?"

The Reason:

(Riddle answer: because he "bugged" him)

Pharaoh thought Moses was bugging him, but stubborn old Pharaoh was really the one clogging up the works.

- Name the nine plagues you have read about to date.
- Are there bugs in your life that are causing problems in your family? Be honest.
- What can you do to debug the works?

Instructions for Holy Ghost bug spray:
Open your heart, kneel down, and pray.

74

The Fire Escape

In a cold dark room you have a candle, an oil lamp, and a fireplace. You only have one match. Which do you light first?

Key Verse:
How shall we escape if we neglect so great a salvation? (Hebrews 2:3).

Scripture Reading:
Exodus 12:1-14

Holly jumped up and down and spun around and around.

"Calm down," big brother Josh ordered as he sat his suitcase by the front door.

"Here they come! Here they come!" shouted Holly.

Mrs. Wright came to the door just as Uncle Mark and Aunt Angie drove into the driveway. "I'm glad you're here," she laughed as they got out of the car. "I think Holly would have exploded in five more minutes."

"Let's go," ordered Josh as he and Holly jumped into the back seat.

"Where's your suitcase?" Uncle Mark asked. "You might need your toothbrush."

Josh grinned as he got out of the car. "Probably not, but I do need my money. And it's in my suitcase."

"You'd better kiss your mother goodbye," Aunt Angie reminded Holly. "You won't see her again for three days."

A cloudy look crossed the little girl's face. Mrs. Wright grinned as she stuck her head in the car window. "Don't cry, honey. You'll have a wonderful time in the mountains. Don't forget to bring me something!"

"Bye, Mom." Josh threw his mother a kiss as he tossed their suitcases into the trunk.

Aunt Angie asked, "Josh, how would you like to sit in the front with Uncle Mark? I'll ride in the back with Holly."

Josh grinned. "Sure. He may need me to read the map. I learned how last year in social studies."

Mrs. Wright winked at her sister, Angie. "If Josh reads the map, it may be a long time before I see you again."

Holly's smile faded. "Mommy, I. . . ."

Aunt Angie hugged the little girl. "Your mother was only teasing, honey. We'll be back in three days. Promise."

"Let's go, Uncle Mark. Three days isn't long. We don't have time to waste." Josh fiddled with the seat controls.

The next hours were spent singing, laughing, and playing games as the car sped toward the mountains. "We'll stop in the next town and eat. Then we'll get a motel for the night," Uncle Mark planned.

Later, after they checked into their room, Josh pointed at the door. "Look at this. It's a map of the motel. We're right here in this room marked X."

Uncle Mark walked across the room. "It's a fire escape plan," he explained. "We need to study it."

Holly's voice quivered, "Is there going to be a fire?"

"I hope not," Uncle Mark replied. "But we would be smart to know the escape route. I'll read the instructions to you."

As Holly listened, her face grew longer. "I want to g-g-go home," she wailed.

"Read it to yourself, Mark. You're scaring Holly," Aunt Angie cautioned as she gathered the little girl in her arms. "Listen to me, honey. I've stayed in lots and lots of motels, and I have never had to use the fire escape."

"Don't worry," Uncle Mark said in his teasing voice. "If there's a fire, your old Uncle Mark will take care of you. He knows the way outta here."

Holly looked up at her uncle. "Mamma said that I don't have to be scared of Hell either. She said Jesus will take care of me."

Uncle Mark pinched her cheek gently. "He sure will. He's made an escape route for us. If we follow Him, He'll lead us to safety."

The Reason:
(Riddle answers: the match)

When the Israelites applied the blood of the lamb on the doors of their houses, they were saved from death. When we repent, are baptized in Jesus' name, and receive the Holy Ghost, the blood of the Lamb of God (Jesus) is applied to our hearts. It's our fire escape.

- Have you obeyed Acts 2:38? If not, don't delay any longer.

If from sin you need out,
Follow God's escape route.

The Repellent

Where can you find ticks in your house?

Key Verse:
And when I see the blood, I will pass over you (Exodus 12:13).

Scripture Reading:
Exodus 12:29-36

"We're going fishing, Mom," Bradley called through the kitchen door as he collected his fishing gear from the garage. "Would you fix us a couple of sandwiches, please?"

In a few minutes Mrs. Short came out the door. She handed the boys a lunch sack, a thermos, and a can of bug spray. "Use this first. The ticks are bad this year."

"Sure." Bradley shuddered. "I hate ticks."

"Be back by dinner." Mrs. Short returned to the house. Bradley rolled up his sleeves and began spraying.

"Yuk!" his city cousin Trent turned up his nose. "That stinks. I'd rather be bitten by ticks than smell like that."

Bradley frowned. "Ticks can be dangerous, even deadly."

Trent shrugged. "I'll take my chances."

Later as the boys relaxed in the shade and waited for the fish to bite, Trent pulled a plastic bag from his pocket. "How'd you like to get high?" he asked.

"High?" Bradley repeated. "You mean on drugs?"

"Well, it's not really drugs," Trent hedged. "It's just my mom's diet pills. They won't hurt you, just add a little zip to the day."

"No, thanks," Bradley replied firmly. "I like the day as it is."

"Awwww, don't be a wimp." Trent reached for the thermos.

"I'm not a wimp. I'm a Christian." Bradley stood up. "And if you're going to pop pills, you'll do it alone." He began reeling in his line.

"But we haven't caught any fish yet." Bradley didn't reply. Trent relented, "Awww, don't leave. I won't pop any pills. Promise."

Bradley looked him in the eye. "I'm not staying as long as you have those pills."

With a disgusted look, Trent flung the pills into the pond. "There. Does that satisfy you?"

Without a word, Bradley cast his line back into the water and sat down. After several minutes silence, Trent asked, "How could you do that?"

"Do what?" Bradley asked.

"Say no." Trent snapped his fingers. "Just like that."

"It was easy," Bradley answered. "I've been covered by the blood of Jesus."

Trent did a double take. "The what?"

"The blood of Jesus," Bradley repeated. "When I repented, was baptized in Jesus' name, and filled with the Holy Ghost, I was covered by His blood."

Trent shuddered. "Sounds gruesome to me."

Bradley grinned. "Well, it's not. It's great." He picked up the can of bug spray. "Just like this spray repels bugs, the blood of Jesus repels sin. It's easy to say no to sin when you have no desire for it."

Trent's voice trembled, "If I was covered by Jesus' blood, would I quit wanting pills? I'm scared I'm getting hooked."

Bradley nodded. "The blood of Jesus will wash away the desire for them. It'll make you new, man."

Trent looked at his feet. "Uhho! What's that little bug crawling up my sock?"

Bradley leaned closer. "It's a tick. Better get him quick!" He handed Trent the can of spray.

Trent uncapped it and gave the bug a big dose. "That takes care of him." He rolled up his sleeves. "Guess I'd better use this stuff after all. And when we get back to the house, maybe your mother will tell me more about the blood of Jesus."

The Reason:

(Riddle answer: in the clock, tick-tock)

Because of the blood of the lamb, the Israelites escaped death.
- Why do you think Jesus is called the Lamb of God?
- Have you had Jesus' blood applied to your life by repenting, being baptized in His name, and being filled with the Holy Ghost?
- Name some sins that the blood of Jesus repels (drives out) of our lives.

Jesus' blood will cover you
So that sin cannot get through.

76

No Way Out

What was the weather like when Israel camped before the Red Sea?

Key Verse:
When you pass through the waters, I will be with you (Isaiah 43:2).

Scripture Reading:
Exodus 14:10-28

Kristi was so excited. Uncle Bob's family had moved to Centerville. Now she could be friends with Melinda.

"I hope so," Mrs. Jackson said gently. "But they aren't Christians. You may not have much in common with Melinda."

"But we're the same age, in the same grade, and even have the same last name," Kristi said. "And we're cousins."

As soon as they were settled in their new home, Melinda invited Kristi to spend the night with her.

"I'll bring my new game," Kristi said.

"OK," Melinda agreed, "but we may not have time to play it. I think my dad has a special surprise planned for us."

After school the girls talked and talked and talked. At the dinner table, Aunt Sue smiled, "I believe we have a couple of chatterboxes in the family."

Uncle Bob pushed his chair back and grinned. Melinda saw her dad's expression. "Oh! I just remembered the surprise. What is it, Dad?"

Her father pulled four tickets out of his wallet. "Tickets to a professional ball game. I haven't been in several years."

Kristi's heart slowed. "But . . . but. . . ."

Uncle Bob looked at her. "But what? You didn't wear your jeans? You can borrow . . . oh, I forgot; you don't wear jeans." He cleared his throat. "Well, no matter. You're wearing a jean skirt."

Kristi blinked. "But, Uncle Bob, I . . . we . . . we don't go to professional ball games."

"You don't like ball games?" he asked in amazement. "Well, won't hurt you to do one thing you don't like. You'll do it for your old Uncle Bob, won't you?"

"But we don't believe we should go to games like that," Kristi blurted out. "There's drinking and cussing and . . . and. . . ."

"There's drinking and cussing everywhere." Uncle Bob brushed her excuse aside. "One game won't pollute you."

Tears filled Kristi's eyes. "I'd better call my mom." After eight rings, she slowly hung up.

"So they're not home," Uncle Bob said. He put his arm around the little girl. "You tried. Don't worry about it, honey. I'll make it okay with your folks. I'm not about to miss this game after paying big bucks for the tickets. We leave in thirty minutes."

With a heavy heart, Kristi helped Aunt Sue clear the table. *O, Lord Jesus,* she prayed silently. *What am I going to do? I don't want to go, but there's no way out.*

Aunt Sue hugged Kristi gently. "Better borrow one of Melinda's jackets. It will be cool." As Kristi went toward the door, Aunt Sue added, "Honey, please try to enjoy yourself. Uncle Bob planned this for you."

As they put on their jackets, the phone rang. Aunt Sue answered it. "Hello. Oh, hi, Mary . . . Yes, they're having a great time. . . . Oh, I'm sorry to hear that. . . . We were just going out the door. . . . Yes, I guess we can. . . . OK. See you in a few minutes. Bye."

Aunt Sue gave Kristi a crooked smile. "That was your mother. She's been called in to work. She needs you to come home and take care of the baby."

Kristi ran up the stairs to get her overnight bag. "Next time I spend the night with Melinda," she whispered to herself, "we'll spend it at my house."

Then she ran to the car humming, *I know the Lord has made a way for me.*

The Reason:

(Riddle answer: cloudy and windy. See Exodus 14:19, 21.)

Israel was surrounded—a sea in front, mountains on both sides, and the Egyptian army behind. There was no way out. But God made a way where there was no way.

- How did God make a way for the Israelites? for Kristi?
- Have you ever been in a situation where you didn't know what to do next? Did God help you? How?

When you don't know what to do,
Ask the Lord to see you through.

77

Pulling Up Roots

What flower is a part of the eye?

Key Verse:
[Look] diligently . . . lest any root of bitterness springing up cause trouble (Hebrews 12:15).

Scripture Reading:
Exodus 15:22-27

"I just pulled these last week," Jacob muttered as he tugged halfheartedly at the weeds in his mother's flower bed.

His mind was not on his job. It was whirling with ugly, bitter thoughts. His heart felt as dirty as his hands. He jumped to his feet. "Dad's the one with a dirty heart!"

Muffins rubbed against his leg and purred softly. This touch of sympathy unleashed the tears that flowed so easily these days.

Coming out the front door, Mrs. Adams saw Jacob's face. "Oh, son," she cried as she held out her arms.

With a sob Jacob turned from her and stumbled into the house. Behind him he heard his mother praying, "O

God, help us. Help us all . . . Jacob and me and . . . and Martin."

Martin was Jacob's dad. He had packed his bags and moved out two weeks ago. "Your God means more to you than I do!" he had flung at his wife as he slammed the door. But Jacob knew the problem: alcohol meant more to him than his family.

In his room Jacob beat his pillow. "I hate him! I hate him! I hope he never comes back." When his anger was spent, he lay quietly thinking about his mother.

"Don't be bitter, son," she had said. "Be patient. Your dad loves us. He'll be back."

When Jacob's anger was spent, he went to finish his job and found his mother doing it. She was using a garden tool to uproot the weeds. "Better now?" she asked.

Jacob nodded. He knelt beside her and pulled up a weed. It snapped off at ground level. Mrs. Adams said, "If you would get the roots, son, we wouldn't have to do this again next week." Jacob looked doubtful. His mother continued, "When you leave the roots, the weeds sprout again in a few days. When you pull them up by the roots, there is nothing left to sprout. It's a little more work the first time, but it saves lots of time in the long run."

Jacob went to the garage for a tool. When he returned, they worked in comfortable silence. Jacob loved his mother so much. How could his dad treat her so badly?

When they finished, Jacob stretched his cramped muscles. "It sure looks better with the weeds gone."

"It certainly does," Mrs. Adams agreed as she sat down on the porch step. "Son, your dad is unhappier than we are. He is alone; we have each other. He is bound by alcohol; we are free from sin. He needs our love and prayers. The Bible talks about 'a root of bitterness.' To be bitter will only make you have an ugly spirit. Please, Jacob, don't let bitterness grow in your heart." Her voice wavered, "You're such a good, loving boy that I couldn't stand for you to become bitter and hard."

Jacob thought a moment. Then he gave his mother a crooked smile and went into the house. He had to find a quiet corner where he could do a little digging in the garden of his heart.

The Reason:
(Riddle answer: iris)

Bitterness is an ugly weed that will cause beautiful flowers like love and joy to die. Prayer is the tool that digs bitterness up by the roots.
- Do you have hard feelings in your heart against anyone? What are you going to do about it?
- What did Moses do to make the bitter waters of Marah sweet?
- What can you do to make your bitter feelings better?

Only change one letter
To make bitter better.

78

Oatmeal? Again?

What did the little squirrel say when he saw his breakfast?

Key Verse:
And my God shall supply all your need according to His riches in glory by Christ Jesus (Philippians 4:19).

Scripture Reading:
Exodus 16:3-15

"Oatmeal? Again?" Nick turned up his nose as he sat down. "Why can't we have some of those pop-up toast 'ems?"

"Or a doughnut?" his sister Natalie joined the protest.

"Oatmeal is good for you," Mrs. Isaacs replied. "Granddad, would you give thanks?"

After the prayer, Natalie whined, "Could I have some brown sugar for my oatmeal? Please?" Her mother frowned but nodded.

"Did I ever tell you about the time when we had only potatoes to eat for two weeks?" Granddad asked.

Nick shook his head. "No. Did I ever tell you about the time we had oatmeal every morning for two weeks?"

Oatmeal? Again?

Everyone laughed.

Granddad poured milk on his oatmeal. "I was about your age, Nick, when my parents went to pastor a little country church in Idaho. There wasn't much money, but lots of potatoes. Everyone paid their tithes in potatoes. We had potatoes three times a day."

Natalie spooned brown sugar on her oatmeal. "At least we don't have oatmeal three times a day." She grinned. "Although I could eat oatmeal cookies three times a day."

"Easy on the brown sugar, Natalie," Mother instructed.

Granddad cleared his throat. "Back to the potatoes. We didn't even have any butter to put on them. So one day my mother prayed, 'God, I thank You for potatoes, but could You, please, send us some butter?' Late that evening my dad heard mooing at the back door, and there was a strange cow. It was too late to look for the owner, so Dad put the cow in our empty barn. Of course, he milked it. That night we had potato soup. Boy, was it good."

Natalie buttered her toast. "I like potato soup if it has lots of butter in it."

Grandfather shook his head. "We still didn't have any butter. The next morning Dad milked the cow again. And by then there was enough cream to churn."

"Churn? What's that?" Nick asked.

Grandfather explained, "That's when you make butter out of cream."

"Your mamma's prayer was answered," Natalie cheered. "She got her butter."

"Yes," Grandfather smiled. "And there's more. As Dad was putting on his coat to go look for the cow's owner, a man knocked at the door. He was looking for his cow. Before he left, he gave Dad five dollars—a lot of money in those days. We never saw the man or the cow again."

"Was he an angel?" Nick asked.

Grandfather shrugged. "I've often wondered. I do know that cow was a gift from heaven. From then on things got better. I learned a lesson in faith that day that I have never forgotten."

Natalie wrinkled her nose at him. "Do you think things would get better for us if I prayed?"

Grandfather chuckled, "I don't think things are too bad for you right now. You should pray a prayer of thanksgiving." He stood up. "I need to get my car serviced. Why don't I drop you kids off at school." He winked at the children's mother. "Seems like there's a doughnut shop on the way."

Mrs. Isaacs laughed, "Which goes to show you that God not only supplies our needs, He often gives us our wants."

Nick pushed back his empty bowl. "And sometimes He uses grandpas to do it!"

The Reason:

(Riddle answer: "Oh, nuts!")

God not only delivered the Israelites from Egypt, He also provided their needs for the journey to Canaan.
- What are some ways God provided for the Israelites?
- Give thanks for a time God provided your needs.
- Then give thanks for something you have to eat that you don't like.

Millions in the wilderness God did feed,
So don't you think He can supply your need?

79

Frozen Pipe

What is grandmother's favorite rock?

Key Verse:
You called in trouble, and I delivered you; . . . I proved you at the waters of Meribah (Psalm 81:7).

Scripture Reading:
Exodus 17:1-7

Bruce shivered as he crossed the cold floor to the bathroom. How he hated to leave his warm bed on these icy winter mornings! Well, he'd feel better after he washed the sleep from his eyes. He turned on the faucet. Nothing happened. He twisted it again. Nothing.

"Mother," he called. "What's wrong with the water?"

Mrs. Dean came to the door. "The pipes are frozen."

"How will I get ready for school?"

"The best you can," Mrs. Dean answered.

That afternoon when Bruce came home, the pipes were still frozen. "The weatherman says it will be several days before it gets above zero," Mrs. Dean sighed.

"Can't you call a plumber?" Bruce asked.

He was sorry he had asked when he saw the hurt look in his mother's eyes. "You know we can't afford that, son."

"But what are we going to do?" Bruce wailed. "We can't do anything without water!"

Mrs. Dean smiled grimly. "Guess we'll rough it."

Bruce grunted. Then he thought of something. "I read about these airmen who were forced down in the Pacific during the war," he told his mother. "They were dying of thirst as a little cloud, the only one in the sky, passed over them. It was their only hope for water, so they prayed. And, Mom, believe it or not, as they prayed that cloud stopped, changed direction, and came right back over them. And then guess what?" Bruce's eyes were sparkling.

Mrs. Dean whispered, "What?"

Bruce shouted, "It rained!" He dropped to his knees beside the couch. "Let's pray for water.

"Well . . . okay," Mrs. Dean said slowly. "I guess. . . ." She stopped. Bruce was already praying.

The "amen" was barely off his lips before there was a knock at the door. Brother Carpenter, Bruce's scout troop leader from church, stood there. In his hand he carried a toolbox. "Pipes frozen?" he asked Mrs. Dean.

She nodded. "How did you know?"

"It wasn't hard. Everyone's pipes are frozen. I knew you didn't have anyone to thaw yours, so here I am." Brother Carpenter grinned at Bruce. "Get your coat and gloves, son. I need an extra pair of hands, and you could use a little lesson in plumbing."

As Bruce went for his coat, Mrs. Dean smiled at the man standing before her. "I've just been taught a great lesson in faith. Thanks for answering our prayer, Brother Carpenter."

The Reason:
(Riddle answer: her rocking chair)

Out of a dry, old rock God provided water for a multitude of people and their animals. What a gusher that must have been!
- Do you have a special need? Have you prayed about it?
- Has God answered a prayer for you recently? Tell someone about it.
- In sixty seconds, how many uses can you think of for water? Thank God for water!

Out of an old, dry rock,
God gave water to His flock.

80

Behind the Scenes

When was the first holdup in the Bible?

Key Verse:
But you, be strong and do not let your hands be weak, for your work shall be rewarded! (II Chronicles 15:7).

Scripture Reading:
Exodus 17:8-16

"That Jason makes me so mad!" Bart exploded as he came into the kitchen.

Mrs. Parks looked up from turning the steaks. "Oh?"

"He's always bragging about this or that. Just because his dad is the preacher, he thinks he's somebody special. He's Jason Martin, the PK." Bart plopped down at the table. "I wish Dad was a preacher, instead of a factory worker."

Mrs. Parks laughed, "Well, I don't. I'm perfectly happy to be married to a member of the board of trustees."

"Yeah, but nobody even knows Dad's a trustee. He's never up front like Jason's dad. We are just saints in Jason's dad's church."

"Being a saint is the highest calling in the world," Mrs. Parks said firmly.

Bart didn't believe her. "I wish our family was. . . ."

Melissa burst into the kitchen. "Guess what? Our class is going to put on an Easter drama."

"Wonderful," Mrs. Parks replied.

"What are you going to be?" Bart asked.

"I'm in charge of collecting the props and painting the scenery," Melissa announced proudly.

"Oh, brother!" Bart drawled. "If I was in it, I'd want to be Jesus, or at least Peter."

"We know," Mrs. Parks responded drily. "You like the spotlight. Now, go wash. Dinner is almost ready."

The weeks passed. Melissa worked excitedly on the Easter drama. Bart moped around the house, criticizing everything and everybody as jealousy ate at him like a cancer.

The night of the drama Bart sat pouting with his parents toward the back of the sanctuary while the Martin family sat on the front row. "He's always up front," Bart muttered.

But once the drama started, Bart forgot everything else. It was so real. He forgot that Peter was George Smith and Judas was John Martin. He was ashamed to find tears rolling down his cheeks until he heard his dad blow his nose loudly. Then when "Jesus" rose from the dead, Bart was on his feet, along with everyone else. When the final curtain fell, it took him a minute to remember where he was.

Following the program Pastor Martin took the stage. After congratulating the cast on their performance, he said, "Now I want Melissa Parks to come out here."

With her color high, Melissa came from behind the curtains. Pastor Parks put a hand on her shoulder. "This little gal has worked harder than anyone," he said with a smile. "One reason this drama seemed so real was the fantastic costumes and background scenery. I want you to give her a special round of applause."

Instantly, the crowd was back on their feet with Bart clapping loudest of all.

On the way home Bart listened silently to Melissa's cheerful chatter. As Mr. Parks turned the car into the driveway, Bart said quietly, "You don't have to be in the spotlight to be important, do you?" Before anyone could answer, he continued, "I'm proud of you, Melissa, and . . . and you, too, Dad."

And once again, Bart was surprised to hear his dad blow his nose loudly.

The Reason:

(Riddle answer: when Aaron and Hur held up Moses' hands)

It takes a lot of people behind the scenes to win a battle, to stage a drama, and to operate a church.
- What part did Moses, Aaron, and Hur play in Israel's victory over the Amalekites?
- Name three people in your church who work behind the scenes to keep your church going. Write a thank-you note today to one of them.

Many victories are won behind the scene
By important people who are seldom seen.

Inside the Fence

How are rules like a fence?

Key Verse:
And the Lord commanded us to observe all these statutes, to fear the LORD our God, for our good always (Deuteronomy 6;24).

Scripture Reading:
Exodus 20:1-20

"I don't know why I can't go to Marilynda's swimming party," Cassie complained on the way home from the store.

Mrs. Daniels sighed, "Yes, you do. You know we don't believe in boys and girls going swimming together."

"'We don't believe in this; we don't believe in that,'" Cassie mimicked. "Why do Christians have so many rules? People in the world do everything they want to do."

"No one does everything they want to do," Mrs. Daniels replied as the car rolled into the garage. "Everyone is a servant, either to God or to sin. Help me carry these groceries into the house, please."

The phone was ringing when they entered the kitchen. As Mrs. Daniels picked up the receiver, Cassie said, "I'm going to go outside and play with Happy."

Mrs. Daniels was just hanging up the phone when Cassie burst into the kitchen. "Mother! Happy's gone! He crawled under the fence again."

"I know," Mrs. Daniels answered. "That was the dog pound. They have him. To get him, we'll have to pay his fine, twenty-five dollars."

"Wow!" Cassie whistled.

"I've got fifteen dollars," Mrs. Daniels said. "Do you have ten?"

Cassie nodded slowly. "I think so. I was saving for a new tennis racket, but we have to get Happy. . . ." The words trailed off as she left the room.

Later on the way home from the dog pound, Cassie scolded, "Happy, you naughty puppy! Why did you run away? Look how much you cost us! Don't you know it's not safe outside the fence?"

Happy wagged his tail and licked Cassie's nose. He was so glad to be free that he didn't mind being scolded. Mrs. Daniels tapped the horn and Cassie looked up to see her Uncle Martin pass them in his delivery truck.

"Uncle Martin sure has changed since he got in church," Cassie remarked. "He's got a job, and he smiles all the time."

Mrs. Daniels nodded. "When Martin was a boy, he didn't appreciate the church; he thought it was a bunch of rules made up to keep him from having fun. So he quit going to church and started running with the wrong crowd. He thought he was free. And he was for a little while. But soon he was bound by tobacco, alcohol, and drugs. Remember what he said the other night?"

Cassie nodded. "Yes. He said he didn't know what bondage was until sin got a hold of him."

"Yes, and he said, 'Now that I'm back in church, I know what freedom really is,'" Mrs. Daniels quoted.

Cassie hugged her puppy. "Happy ought to appreciate his big yard now, after being cooped up in that dirty, little pen."

Mrs. Daniels nodded, "Yes, just like Uncle Martin appreciates the church. He realizes now that the rules are for our protection, not to enslave us."

Cassie held Happy up in front of her face. "Happy," she said, "I want you to remember that the fence is to keep you out of trouble, not to keep you from having fun."

Cassie met her mother's eyes in the rear-view mirror. She nodded, "I'll remember, too."

The Reason:

(Riddle answer: They keep us out of trouble.)

When God delivered Israel from Egyptian bondage, He didn't set them free to do everything they wanted to do. They still had rules to obey.

- Why did God give Israel the Ten Commandments?
- Cassie and her mother paid Happy's fine. How did Jesus pay the "fine" for our sins?
- Why is it better to be God's servant than Satan's? Whose servant are you?

God's laws are good for me.
When I obey them, I am free.

82

Sharla's Idol

How were the Israelites handicapped?

Key Verse:
"You shall have no other gods before Me" (Exodus 20:3).

Scripture Reading:
Exodus 32:1-20

As the miles passed, Sharla chattered cheerfully. Her conversation was peppered with "Judith said this" and "Judith said that"; "Judith did this" and "Judith did that."

"Who is Judith?" Mr. Andrews asked.

"Oh, she's the most popular girl in school," Sharla replied. "Last year she didn't know I was on the earth. But this year we're best friends."

"Hummmmm," Mrs. Andrews said. "Could your dad's promotion at the bank and our new home have anything to do with that?"

Sharla shrugged. "Maybe. How far to Uncle Joe's?"

"About fifty miles."

Sharla flipped her long, dark hair back. With a thumping heart she began, "Mother, my hair is so hot and heavy. I . . . I . . . could I uhhhhh . . . I mean, Judith said if I would just trim the edges a little to even it up, it would look so much neater and uhhhhh . . ." She trailed to a stop.

"Sharla, your hair is your glory. It's beautiful."

"But it's so much trouble and . . . and not in style."

"Have you asked God about cutting your hair?" Mr. Andrews joined the conversation. Sharla was shocked. "Of course not."

"Just Judith," Mr. Andrews responded drily. "You know why we can't allow you to cut your hair, Sharla. God's Word teaches that women are to have long hair. When you get God to change His Word, we'll change our minds."

Sharla pushed into a corner of the back seat to pout.

After a few miles Mrs. Andrews handed her a Bible. "Why don't you study your Bible club memory work?"

"I'm going to drop out of Bible club," Sharla said.

"Drop out?" Mrs. Andrews was shocked. "But you love it."

"Well, I used to. Now I have so many other things, I really don't have time. Judith said . . . uhhhhh . . . well, anyway, I think I'll quit."

"What did Judith say?" Mr. Andrews asked.

"Oh, uhhhh . . . nothing important."

"I want to know what she said," Mr. Andrews pressed. Sharla frowned. "She said Bible club was kid stuff and now that we're in middle school we're too old for it."

With a tight voice Mrs. Andrews said, "You are not dropping out of Bible club, Sharla. Now work on the Ten Commandments. They're in Exodus 20." Her tone of voice told Sharla that she had said enough—in fact, too much.

"'You shall have no other gods before Me,'" Sharla read. "That doesn't even apply to us. We don't worship idols."

Mr. Andrews turned on the air conditioner. "Don't be too sure. Anything we put before God is an idol. It can be clothes or money or a job—or even another person."

When they arrived, Uncle Joe and Aunt Bonnie came out to meet them, followed by their daughter Tina. Sharla was shocked at the way her cousin looked. She had the craziest hairdo, and her clothes were wild.

As the girls entered Tina's room, Sharla blinked. There were posters everywhere of the latest rock star, Monica. And Tina looked just like her! The walls were vibrating with the sounds of Monica's latest recording. *Boy,* Sharla thought, *I'm glad we're just staying overnight.*

By the time they said their goodbyes the next afternoon, Sharla was disgusted. As they rolled down the driveway, she exploded, "I'm sick of hearing-about Monica, the wonderful, the marvelous, the beautiful! Tina tries to walk like her, sing like her, look like her. She even eats the same cereal! Yuck! Tina has made a god out of Monica. Her whole life revolves around what Monica says and does. Monica is Tina's idol!"

Mr. Andrews turned the car onto the highway. "Now you know how we can have idols."

"I sure do," Sharla replied. "Judith said that Mon. . . ." Sharla's voice trailed off.

"What did Judith say?" Mrs. Andrews asked.

Sharla shook her head. "Never mind. It's not important. Would you hand me the Bible, Mother? I need to learn the rest of the Ten Commandments for Bible club."

The Reason:
(Riddle answer: They had stiff necks.)

There is only one God. We are not to worship anything or anybody else.
- What kind of idol did the Israelites make? Why?
- Is it possible to worship an idol and not realize it? How was Sharla doing this?
- Name five things that people worship.

Anything can an idol be,
If it stands between God and me.

83

Following Instructions

How do we know Moses was an usher?

Key Verse:
For we are God's fellow workers; . . . you are God's building (I Corinthians 3:9).

Scripture Reading:
Exodus 25:1-9; 31:1-6; 40:2, 33

"I don't know how this workshop gets so cluttered," Mr. Wright mumbled as he divided the things to keep from the throwaways.

"Can I have some scrap pieces of lumber, Dad?" Jeremy sorted through the throwaways. "To build a birdhouse."

"I suppose so," Mr. Wright answered as he added a small square of plywood to the pile.

Jeremy grabbed it. "That'll make a good floor."

"Let me help." Megan picked up a hammer.

"No way," Jeremy declared. "This is my own individual, special project. I don't want help from anybody. You want a birdhouse? Build your own."

"I don't know how. I just wanted to help," Megan pouted.

"You can help me, Megan." Mr. Wright handed her a broom.

"I need some nails." Jeremy rummaged through a drawer.

Mr. Wright picked out a box of nails. "These should be the right size."

As they worked, Jeremy told his dad, "I invited Mr. Marker to our revival. But he said he didn't need anyone telling him how to live."

Megan stopped her broom in midair. "He doesn't even have a Bible. He said he tried to read the Bible one time, but it didn't make sense to him. He said he doesn't need it anyway."

"He ought to go to church and listen to Pastor Wise. Then he could understand it." Jeremy handed a board to his dad. "This board is too long. Would you saw it for me?"

"How long do you want it?" Mr. Wright asked.

Jeremy motioned with his hands. "About this long."

Mr. Wright grinned as he sawed one end off of the board.

"Thanks, Dad." Jeremy fit the board to another one. "Now this other one is too short," he grumbled. He rummaged through the throwaway pile again and pulled out another board. "This one should be about right."

"What size birdhouse are you building?" Mr. Wright asked.

Jeremy shrugged. "Big enough for a bird's nest, I guess."

His father reached up on a top shelf and took down a big, blue book. "I think there is a pattern for a birdhouse in this manual." He flipped through the book.

Jeremy looked at the instructions. "That looks too hard. I want to build a birdhouse by myself without any help from anyone or any instructions."

Father nodded and put the book up. They worked in silence for several minutes. Then Jeremy handed his dad a board. "Could you drill a hole in this one for the birds to go in and out?"

"I could," Mr. Wright answered, "but I thought you wanted to build it by yourself."

"But I can't use the drill," Jeremy whined.

"I know," Father replied. "The truth is, Jeremy, you can't build a birdhouse by yourself. You need help. And if I am going to help you, I need some instructions." Mr. Wright took down the book again. "You can save yourself a lot of frustration and time if you will accept help and follow instructions."

Jeremy looked at the mismatched pieces around him and nodded.

"When Moses built the Tabernacle, he had to follow the instructions God gave him," Mr. Wright reminded.

"And he had to have help, too," Megan added. "Lots of help."

"OK," Jeremy opened the blue book. "I get the point."

The Reason:

(Riddle answer: He took up an offering.)

- How was Jeremy acting like Mr. Marker?
- Why is it important that we follow instructions?
- Can you think of something difficult you have been able to do lately because someone helped you?

Whatever God's Word says, obey,
And He will help you every day.

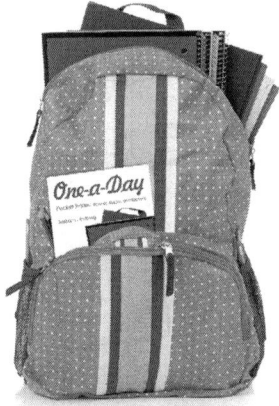

84

Brother Trouble

Who was the first baby sitter in the Bible?

Key Verse:
Obey those who rule over you, and be submissive (Hebrews 13:17).

Scripture Reading:
Numbers 12:1-16

Rodney hated being the middle child. "Either Kara's ordering me around, or I'm baby-sitting Mark," he complained as he sat beside Grandpa Nelson on the porch step.

Grampa nodded. "Yep, I know the feelin'. I was a middle kid, too. Never could decide if I was the baby or the baby sitter."

Rodney grinned at the thought of Gramps being a baby. Then he frowned as he saw Kara coming through the hedge. "Here she comes now to give me orders."

"Rodney! Rodney!" his big sister called. "Come home. You have to baby sit with Mark while we go to the store."

"Who said?" Rodney demanded.

"Mother!" Kara turned back to the house.

Rodney made a face at her back. "See what I told you?" Slowly he got to his feet and ambled across the lawn. He might have to obey, but he sure wasn't going to hurry.

"Mark is playing in his swimming pool," Mrs. Rice said. "Just watch him until we get back. We won't be long."

Without a word Rodney went into the back yard.

"Look at me, Rodney," four-year-old Mark demanded as he lay on his stomach in the shallow pool and flapped his legs and arms in the air. "I'm an ock-a-pus."

"Yeah," Rodney sneered, "and I'm a whale. If you don't be good, I'll whale the daylights out of you."

Mark's face clouded. "That's not nice."

Rodney ignored him and began shooting baskets. Soon he forgot about Mark. Only when the ball bounded toward the pool did he remember.

"What are you doing?" he demanded, although he could plainly see that Mark was carrying dirt from his mother's flower bed and dumping it into his swimming pool.

"I'm buildin' a dam," the little boy answered.

"Look at you!" Rodney scolded. "Boy, Mother's going to be mad! You've messed up her flower bed and your swimming pool, and you look like a mud sculpture."

Two blue eyes peered out at him. "What's a sulpsure?"

"Never mind. Come with me. You've got to have a bath."

"No!" Mark screamed. "I don't want a bath. I want to build a dam."

"Well, that's too bad." Rodney grabbed the little boy's hand. "You've got to take a bath."

"No! No!" Mark screamed. "I don't have to mind you. You're just my brother. You're not my boss!"

"Oh, yes, I am." Rodney pulled the kicking boy toward the house. "Mother told me to take care of you. . . ."

"What in the world?" Mrs. Rice came around the house.

When Rodney dropped Mark's hand, the little boy went running toward his mother. "Rodney thinks he's my boss."

Mrs. Rice backed away. "Don't touch me! You're filthy! And Rodney is your boss when I ask him to watch you."

Tears streaked through the mud on Mark's face. "But he's not my boss. He's just my brother! A bossy brother!"

"When I leave you with Mark, you must obey him," Mrs. Rice said as she attached the water hose to the faucet. "Because he is responsible for you. He has to answer to me for what you do." She handed Rodney the hose. "Here, finish your job."

The Reason:

(Riddle answer: Miriam. See Exodus 2:4.)

God has placed over everyone someone else in authority. When we obey those in authority over us, we are actually obeying God.

- What was wrong with Miriam and Aaron's rebelling against their little brother, Moses?
- Why is it important for you to obey your pastor?
- Compare Rodney's attitude toward Kara with Mark's attitude toward Rodney.
- Do you have a big brother or sister? What is your attitude toward them when they give you a message from your parents?

Obey those in control,
For they watch for your soul.

85

One Step at a Time

What animals lived in Canaan?

Key Verse:
I can do all things through Christ who strengthens me (Philippians 4:13).

Scripture Reading:
Numbers 13:1-2, 17-20, 26-33

"Walk twenty kilometers for Sheaves for Christ? Me? Man, are you crazy? That's over twelve miles!" Alan protested.

Riley shrugged. "So what? We can do it."

"Not me. I've still got a blister on my heel from our boy's club hike." Alan picked up the classified section of the newspaper.

"You just don't want to," Riley said.

Alan ignored him. "I wish I could find a job. Nobody will hire a kid. 'Come back when you're sixteen,' they say. I don't want to wait four years to earn some money."

"I'm going to make some money," Riley told him.

Alan peered over the top of the paper. "How?"

"Get sponsors for the March for Missions."

One Step at a Time

"Bah! I thought you meant you were going to earn some money for yourself."

Riley started for the door. He was getting a bit disgusted with his selfish friend.

"Wait!" Alan called. "Here's a job for us. Listen. 'Wanted: Boys to stack bricks. No age limit. Must be dependable.' That's us."

"Where is it?" Riley asked.

"Out at the old refinery. That's only a couple miles from here. Let's walk over and check it out."

"Can you walk a couple of miles?" Riley teased. "Maybe we'd better ride our bikes. Remember your blister?"

Alan gave his friend a withering look. "My bike has a flat. I'm going. Are you?"

The man was happy to hire the boys. "We pay by the brick," he informed them. "Too many goof-offs for us to pay by the hour. You can start any time." He led them around the building to a huge pile of used bricks. "Stack them over there by the fence."

"Wow!" Riley exclaimed. "We can never. . . ."

Alan poked him in the ribs. "Hush!" he whispered. "Want to lose this job before we get it?" He turned to the man. "We'll start right now."

As the man disappeared around the building, Riley said, "Boy, there's no way we can do this job."

"There certainly is," Alan declared as he picked up a brick. "We'll do it one brick at a time. My Dad says that's the way to do any big job."

Riley grinned slyly. "Any big job? Hummmm . . . guess that's the way to walk twenty kilometers, too . . . one step at a time."

Alan almost dropped his brick. "Oh, you! All right, I'll make a deal with you. You stick with me on this job, and I'll march for missions with you."

Riley grabbed a couple of bricks. "You just made yourself a deal, friend. But I think I'll try two bricks at a time."

The Reason:
(Riddle answer: cows and bees. The land flowed with milk and honey. That doesn't mean milk and honey flowed in streams. It means there was plenty of food in the land.)

God planned for the Israelites to take Canaan one city at a time. When they saw the giants, they forgot how big God was. All they could see was how little they were, and they cried, "We can't do it."
- What is the hardest job you ever had? How did you do it?
- Some people think it is hard to be a Christian. Do you think so? Why or why not?

Whatever job you have to do,
Do it little by little until you're through.

86

The Second Chance

How do we know Joshua was an orphan?

Key Verse:
If you are willing and obedient, you shall eat the good of the land (Isaiah 1:19).

Scripture Reading:
Numbers 14:1-10

"The Lord is talking to someone," the evangelist said, looking straight at Mark. "If you will come to the altar right now, He will fill you with the Holy Ghost."

Mark's mouth was dry and his knees weak. *I don't want to go to the altar . . . not tonight,* he rebelled. *I don't see why I can't get the Holy Ghost right here at my seat. I don't want to pray in front of everybody.*

When the evangelist called the saints in to pray, Mark knelt beside the pew. But for some reason, he couldn't pray.

As he started down the aisle after church, he felt a hand on his shoulder. "Son, why didn't you go to the altar?" the evangelist asked. "If you had obeyed God, you would have received the Holy Ghost."

Mark gulped. Before he could answer, the evangelist turned to greet his parents, and Mark escaped.

Outside, Uncle Jeff—young, single, and lots of fun—drove up beside him. "Want to go to Pizza Hut with me? My treat."

Mark hesitated. "Pizza Hut? We went there last Sunday night. I'd rather go to Taco Bell."

"OK," Uncle Jeff responded. As Mark reached for the door handle, his uncle continued, "Have fun. I'm sure Paul would like to go to Pizza Hut."

Before Mark could respond, Uncle Jeff drove across the parking lot. Mark watched as Paul climbed into the car and they drove down the street.

"Well, I like that!" Mark muttered.

"Like what?" Mrs. Hawthorne asked as she came up behind him.

"Uncle Jeff asked me to go to Pizza Hut with him, and then he took Paul instead," Mark told part of the story.

Mrs. Hawthorne wrinkled her brow. "That's strange."

"Yeah," Mark agreed as he followed his parents to the car. "I didn't say I didn't want to go. I just said I'd rather go to Taco Bell."

Mrs. Hawthorne's brow cleared. "Oh. Knowing you, young man, I suppose you told him that you'd go with him and let him treat you, if he'd go where you wanted to go."

Mark slumped down in the back seat. "Not exactly."

"But that's pretty close," Mr. Hawthorne said as he started the car. "Insisting on doing things your way can cause you to miss out on lots of good things."

"Like the Holy Ghost," Mrs. Hawthorne added. "Did you know Paul received the Holy Ghost tonight?"

Hot tears made tracks down Mark's cheeks. Silently, he prayed, *Lord, please give me another chance, and I promise I'll be the first one in the altar.*

BEEP-BEEP. Mark looked up to see that they had pulled alongside Uncle Jeff's car at a red light. The young man rolled down his window. "Change your mind, Mark?" he called. "How about a pizza? I'll still treat."

Mark looked at his parents. They smiled and nodded. In a flash, he changed cars. As he slid in beside Paul, he grinned at his uncle, "Thanks, Uncle Jeff, for giving me a second chance."

The Reason:

(Riddle answer: He was the "son of *Nun*"/none.)

As the Israelites traveled toward Canaan, God gave them many "second chances." But when they arrived at the border and refused to cross over into the Promised Land, God had enough! "You will wander in the wilderness until everyone over twenty years old, except Joshua and Caleb, have died," He told them. When the people heard this, they decided to go into Canaan, after all. But God said, "No. It's too late." They had used up all their "second chances."

- How had God blessed the Israelites in the wilderness?
- Have you ever missed a blessing (or treat) because you wanted to do things your way?
- Can you think of a time when you were given a "second chance" at school or home or church?

When God says, "Go,"
Never, never say, "No."

87

Keep Out

How do we know the earth has a throat?

Key Verse:
For he is God's minister to you for good (Romans 13:4).

Scripture Reading:
Numbers 16:1-3, 23-35

As soon as the Lyon family drove off the church parking lot, Troy's big sister, Angela, exploded. "What right does Pastor Michaels have to tell the young people to stay away from Brownie's Pizza Barn?"

"The right of a pastor who loves you and will answer to God for you," Mrs. Lyons answered.

Mr. Lyons glanced at his daughter in the rear-view mirror. "You don't have to belong to the FBI to know drugs are being sold there."

Angela shrugged, "So? They're not being sold to me or any of the church kids . . . that I know of."

"Yet," Mrs. Lyons added.

"You said they make better pizzas at the Pizza Stop anyway, Angela," Troy reminded.

She snorted, "We don't go to the Barn for pizzas, dummy. We go because that's the meeting place."

"Then you'll have to find another meeting place," Mr. Lyons said firmly. "Now where shall we eat Sunday dinner?"

The next afternoon Troy was skating on the driveway when his neighbor Pete called across the yard. "I'm going to climb the fence around the transformer down the street."

Troy skidded to a stop. "You can't! It's dangerous."

"Who says I can't?"

"The signs say you can't."

"Ahhhh, those signs are just to keep scaredy cats like you out. I'm not afraid of anything or anybody," Pete boasted. "You coming?"

Troy shook his head. "No way! You could get killed."

"Then don't come, little boy," Pete mocked. "Stay home with Mamma."

Troy ran into the house. "Mother! Mother! Pete's going to climb the fence around the transformer!"

Mrs. Lyons called the police while Troy told Angela what Pete had said. Minutes later they ran into the yard as sirens pierced the air. "Stay here," Mrs. Lyons ordered as she ran down the street.

When she returned, her eyes were red. She gave them a watery smile. "We were almost too late. Pete touched a high-voltage line just as the emergency squad arrived. They think he'll live, but he's badly burned. It will be a long time before he recovers."

"He said he wasn't afraid of anything or anybody," Troy repeated.

Mrs. Lyons sighed. "It's smart to fear some things. 'The fear of the Lord is the beginning of wisdom,'" she quoted.

"Does that mean we're suppose to be afraid of God?" Troy asked.

"Not in the sense that we quake and shake," Mrs. Lyons answered. "Another word for 'fear' is 'respect.'"

"Respect? Like I respect you and Dad?"

Mrs. Lyons nodded. "Yes, and like we respect Pastor Michaels." She looked at Angela who hung her head.

"Boy, Pete sure was dumb to ignore the warning signs," Troy said. "They're all over the fence."

"And there are warning signs all over. . . ."

Angela interrupted, "I know—Brownie's Pizza Barn. I may be stubborn, Mom, but I'm not stupid. I get the point. You don't have to worry about me going to Brownie's again. It's too dangerous."

The Reason:

(Riddle answer: It swallowed up Korah and his followers. See Numbers 16:32.)

Before the judgment of God fell on Korah and his gang, God warned the people to get away from them. Keeping company with those who rebel against the men of God can get you into bad trouble.
- What would have happened to the people if they had refused to get away from Korah's gang?
- Why is it important that you obey your pastor?
- Make a list of things it is smart to fear.

To keep out of trouble, always obey
The man of God who leads the way.

88

Out of Control

What is it: the more you lose, the more you have?

Key Verse:
"Be angry, and do not sin": do not let the sun go down on your wrath (Ephesians 4:26).

Scripture Reading:
Numbers 20:1-12

Butch and Carl rode past William's house chanting, "Wimpy Willie! He's so silly. Wimpy Willie."

William blew up! "I've had enough! All week they've been tormenting me." He picked up a rock and ran out to the street. Taking careful aim, he threw it at Butch's back. The sound of shattering glass and screeching brakes caused William's knees to crumple.

In horror he watched as a familiar form climbed out of a car and marched across the yard toward him. At the same instant his mother came running out of the house.

"What happened?" she cried as she saw her son sitting on the ground. "William, are you hurt?"

"No, he's not," answered a gruff voice. "But he should be." The man stopped and stared. "William? Is that you?"

The boy buried his face in his arms and sobbed. Mrs. Nelson turned to the astonished man. "I'm William's mother, Candice Nelson. What happened?"

"William threw a rock at my car," the man said slowly. He looked around. "At least, it looked like he threw it. But, I can't believe that William would . . . It's just not like him. I'm John Beaver, his math teacher."

The adults waited. William took a deep breath and looked up. He nodded. "Yes, sir, I did it. But . . . but I didn't mean to hit your car. I . . . I didn't see you," he groaned.

"Why did you throw it?" his mother asked.

"I was throwing it at . . . at Butch and Carl," William confessed. The words gushed out. "They have been tormenting me all week. Just now they rode by on their bikes singing, 'Wimpy Willie! He's so silly!' I just couldn't take any more so I threw a rock at them and . . . and. . . ."

"And hit Mr. Beaver's car instead," his mother finished.

"Butch Jones and Carl Stanley?" Mr. Beaver dropped to the grass beside the sobbing boy. William nodded. "No matter what anyone else does, William, it's wrong to lose control of your temper. When you do, you always have to pay."

William looked at the shattered car window. "How much will it cost?" he asked. "I've got some money saved for a bicycle."

Mr. Beaver stood up. "I think my insurance is fifty dollars deductible. I'll have to check and let you know." He pulled the boy to his feet and smiled grimly at his tear-stained face. "Just remember, son: when you allow someone to cause you to lose your temper, you put them in control. You don't want Butch and Carl controlling your actions."

William sniffed. "I know. I acted just like them, and I don't want to do that."

"If you'll remember that, William, it will be the best fifty dollars you'll ever spend." Mr. Beaver stuck out his hand. "Still friends?" he asked.

William's face lit up, and he grabbed the man's hand. "Yes, sir. And, Mr. Beaver, I'm sorry."

Mr. Beaver nodded. "I gathered you were. And I figure this will be the last time Butch and Carl will get control over you."

The Reason:
(Riddle answer: temper)

For many years Moses had listened to the Israelites whining and murmuring. He had led them, warned them, and prayed for them. Finally, he lost his temper. God said, "Speak to the rock." Moses struck it instead. His anger at the people caused him to disobey God.
- What did Moses' temper cost him? (See Numbers 20:12.)
- Have you ever done something in anger that you were sorry for later? Did it cost you anything?
- Name three things you can do to keep from losing your temper.

Temper, temper, out of control
Could cause you to lose your soul.

89

The Grumble Bug

What can you hold without using your hands or ever touching it?

Key Verse:
Nor [let us] murmur, as some of them also murmured (I Corinthians 10:10).

Scripture Reading:
Numbers 21:4-9

"Shelly," Mrs. Vinson called. "Come try on this dress."

Shelly threw down her book and went down the hall. "I was just at the best part of my book," she complained. She slipped on the dress and stood impatiently while her mother pinned the hem up. "I wish these sleeves were longer," she said. "And could you change the collar?"

Mrs. Vinson sighed. "Not now. Turn around a little."

Four-year-old Brandi bounced into the room. "Ooohhhh! That's pretty, Shelly."

Shelly frowned. "I don't like this shade of blue."

"You picked it out," Mrs. Vinson reminded. "There. You can take it off."

"We're going to Grandma's. We're going to Grandma's," Brandi sang. "In the morning. In the morning."

"I hope we don't go too early," Shelly fussed.

As she flounced out of the room, she heard her little sister ask, "Why's Shelly so gripey?"

Her mother's answer followed her: "I think she has been bitten by the grumble bug."

"Did it hurt?" Shelly heard Brandi ask just before she slammed her bedroom door. *Grumble bug indeed!*

The next afternoon as they prepared to leave the farm, Grandmother Nelson handed her son a big sack. "Len, fill this with potatoes from the smokehouse to take home with you. Get some onions, too. But be careful. We killed a black widow spider out there yesterday."

By the time they arrived home Shelly's parents were completely disgusted with her. She had grumbled all day. "This grumbling has got to stop!" Mr. Nelson ordered. "It's become a habit—a bad habit."

"The grumble bug bit Shelly," Brandi told her dad.

Everyone laughed but Shelly. A stubborn look crossed her face. The rest of the day she pouted. But sadly, no one noticed.

One day later in the week Shelly was in her room sulking when her mother screamed. She ran into the kitchen.

Mrs. Nelson was leaning against the cabinet. Her face was pale. Her hands were shaking. She pointed at the potato bin. "There's a black widow spider in there! Brandi, come back here! Don't touch that potato bin!"

"But I wanna see the widow," Brandi protested.

At that moment, Mr. Nelson walked in. When the spider was dead, Mrs. Nelson dropped into a chair. "Just think, I've put my hand in there several times this week."

Mr. Nelson grinned wryly, "And I put the potatoes, spider and all, into the sack."

"I wanta see it," Brandi demanded. Mr. Nelson pointed to the lifeless speck on the dust pan. With her hands clasped behind her back, Brandi bent over the spider. She asked thoughtfully. "Do grumble bugs look like widow spiders?"

"Grumble bugs?" Mr. Nelson repeated. Then he remembered. "I don't know. But they both can make you very sick."

"Spiders make your body sick," Mrs. Nelson explained, being careful not to look at Shelly. "Grumble bugs make your attitude sick."

Brandi put her arm around Shelly. "Then that's why Shelly grumbles. I'm gripey, too, when I'm sick."

And this time everyone laughed, even Shelly. When Shelly hugged her little sister, Brandi smiled. "Shelly's better. She can laugh again."

The Reason:

(Riddle answer: your breath)

The Israelites had a bad habit of grumbling. For some, the results were deadly.
- What happened to the Israelites because they grumbled?
- Have you ever been bitten by the "grumble bug"?
- The best way to get rid of a grumbling spirit is to give thanks. Make a list of ten things for which you are thankful.

To kill ugly grumble bugs
Use thanks, love, and hugs.

Moving Day

Bible Trivia:
1. Who was never born but died?
2. Who was born but never died?

Key Verse:
I go to prepare a place for you (John 14:2).

Scripture Reading:
Deuteronomy 34:1-7

Rrrrinnnggg! "I'll get it," called Keith. "Hello . . . Oh, Dad, hi . . . Mom! Long distance. It's Dad."

Keith listened on an extension phone as his parents talked. "I've found the perfect house, Lisa," his dad said. "Can you be ready to move next weekend?"

"Next weekend?" Mrs. White exclaimed. "I thought we were going to wait until school was out."

"Do we have to?" Mr. White asked. "I'm so lonely without my family."

"I know," Mrs. White agreed. "Keith and I miss you, too."

"What do you say, son?" Mr. White asked. "Would it be all right with you to move before school is out?"

"Sure, Dad. I'm ready to move tomorrow . . . but. . . ."

"What?" Mr. White asked.

"What about Grampa Dawson? I've been trying to find someone to help him, but everyone is too busy."

"God will send Gramps the help he needs when he needs it," Mr. White assured his son. "He has taken care of him for ninety-three years. He won't fail him now."

The next afternoon Keith hopped up the steps of Grampa Dawson's house. "Anybody home?" he called through the door.

"Where else would I be?" laughed Gramps. "Come in, son."

"Dad's coming for us," Keith announced. "We're moving next weekend. Oh, Gramps, I wish you were my real grandpa so you could go with us."

Gramps sighed, "I am going to miss you, Keith. But don't you worry none about me. Your dad needs his family with him. I'll find someone to run my errands and read my mail."

"Just think, we'll be living by the mountains and the ocean both. I can't wait. Maybe someday you can come visit us, Gramps."

Gramps chuckled, "That would be nice."

Later that evening Keith and his mother were packing when the phone rang. "Hello . . . Yes . . . When? . . . Oh, thanks for calling." Slowly she hung up the phone.

Keith rushed to her side. "What's wrong, Mom?" Mrs. White wiped a tear from her cheek. "That was Grampa Dawson's neighbor." She took a deep breath.

"They just found him. He . . . he was on his couch—dead."

"Oh, no!" Keith wailed. "He can't be. I saw him this afternoon. He wasn't even sick."

Mrs. White put a comforting arm around her son. "Remember, he was ninety-three. He must have had a heart attack. You don't have to worry about him anymore, Keith. His Father took him home."

"Like Dad's coming for us?" Keith choked back a sob. Mrs. White looked at the packing crates around them and nodded. "Today was moving day for Gramps."

Tears dripped off Keith's chin onto his shirt. He gave his mother a wavering smile. "I just thought of something. In Heaven Gramps won't need anyone to run his errands and read his mail. He can do it himself."

The Reason:

(Riddle answer: 1. Adam and Eve; 2. Enoch and Elijah)

For the child of God, death is simply moving to a new home.
- What was different about Moses' death and burial?
- Have you ever moved to a new town? What made you sad about moving? What made you happy?
- Has someone you loved died? Draw a picture of them in Heaven.

What a happy moving day,
From earth to Heaven far away.

One-A-Day Pocket Stories

Index

Key Verses

Exodus 8:23
Exodus 12:13
Exodus 20:3
Numbers 24:9
Numbers 32:23
Deuteronomy 4:36
Deuteronomy 6:24
Deuteronomy 11:26
I Kings 8:56
II Chronicles 15:7
Job 23:10
Psalm 16:6
Psalm 17:8
Psalm 19:14
Psalm 27:10
Psalm 34:19
Psalm 37:4
Psalm 37:7
Psalm 51:10
Psalm 54:6
Psalm 75:6-7
Psalm 78:1
Psalm 81:7
Psalm 86:5
Psalm 94:22
Psalm 106:13
Psalm 107:1
Psalm 138:7
Psalm 145:4
Proverbs 6:6
Proverbs 15:3
Proverbs 16:2
Proverbs 16:7
Proverbs 16:9
Proverbs 17:17
Song of Solomon 8:6
Isaiah 1:19
Isaiah 43:2
Isaiah 49:16
Isaiah 59:17
Jeremiah 1:7
Amos 3:3
Matthew 5:9
Matthew 7:7
Matthew 25:21
Matthew 18:20
Luke 6:37
Luke 6:38
Luke 17:26
John 8:36
John 10:10
John 14:2
John 14:18
John 15:13
Romans 5:12
Romans 6:16
Romans 8:28
Romans 11:34
Romans 12:18
Romans 12:21
Romans 13:4
I Corinthians 3:9
I Corinthians 10:10
II Corinthians 2:11
II Corinthians 5:7
II Corinthians 5:17
II Corinthians 6:2
II Corinthians 6:14
Galatians 6:7
Philippians 4:13
Ephesians 4:26
Philippians 4:19
Philippians 4:19
Colossians 3:13
II Timothy 2:22
Hebrews 2:3
Hebrews 10:36
Hebrews 12:15
Hebrews 12:16
Hebrews 13:2
Hebrews 13:17
James 2:9
I Peter 2:9
I Peter 3:16
I John 3:1
I John 3:15
I John 4:4
I John 4:21

Scripture Reading:

Genesis 1:1-13
Genesis 1:14-19
Genesis 1:20-31
Genesis 2:15-23
Genesis 3:1-13
Genesis 3:14-24
Genesis 4:1-6
Genesis 4:9-16
Genesis 5:21-27
Genesis 6:1-8
Genesis 6:9-14; 7:11-17
Genesis 8:1-19
Genesis 8:20-22; 9:8-17
Genesis 11:1-9
Genesis 12:1-9
Genesis 13:2-17
Genesis 14:8-16
Genesis 16:1-16
Genesis 18:1-16
Genesis 18:16-33
Genesis 19:15-30
Genesis 21:1-8
Genesis 21:9-21
Genesis 21:22-34
Genesis 22:1-14
Genesis 23:1-20
Genesis 24:1-4, 10-20
Genesis 24:34-51, 58-67
Genesis 25:29-34
Genesis 26:12-33
Genesis 27:1-29
Genesis 27:30-41
Genesis 28:10-22
Genesis 29:1-14
Genesis 29:15-30
Genesis 30:25-36
Genesis 31:1-7, 17-18, 22-24, 45-49
Genesis 32:1-20
Genesis 32:22-32
Genesis 33:1-16
Genesis 33:1-15
Genesis 35:16-20
Genesis 35:23-27
Genesis 37:1-4
Genesis 37:5-11
Genesis 37:12-36
Genesis 39:1-20
Genesis 39:20-23
Genesis 40:1-23
Genesis 41:1-13
Genesis 41:14-16, 25-44
Genesis 41:46-57
Genesis 42:1-20
Genesis 42:21-38
Genesis 43:1-17, 26-34
Genesis 44:1-18, 30-34
Genesis 45:1-15
Genesis 45:16-28; 46:26-30
Genesis 48:1-22
Genesis 50:15-21
Exodus 1:8-14
Exodus 1:22; 2:1-10
Exodus 2:11-15
Exodus 3:1-10
Exodus 4:10-18
Exodus 5:1-9, 22-23
Exodus 7:7-13
Exodus 7:14-25
Exodus 8:1-15
Exodus 8:16-24
Exodus 9:1-12
Exodus 9:13-26
Exodus 10:12-23
Exodus 12:1-14
Exodus 12:29-36
Exodus 14:10-28
Exodus 15:22-27
Exodus 16:3-15
Exodus 17:1-7
Exodus 17:8-16
Exodus 20:1-20
Exodus 32:1-20
Exodus 25:1-9; 31:1-6; 40:2, 33
Numbers 12:1-16
Numbers 13:1-2, 17-20, 26-33
Numbers 14:1-10
Numbers 16:1-3, 23-35
Numbers 20:1-12
Numbers 21:4-9
Deuteronomy 34:1-7
Mark 12:18-34—20